Werewolves

Fact or Fiction?

Angela Cybulski, *Book Editor*

Bruce Glassman, *Vice President*
Bonnie Szumski, *Publisher*
Scott Barbour, *Managing Editor*

OPPOSING
VIEWPOINTS®
SERIES

GREENHAVEN
PRESS®

THOMSON
———*———
GALE

San Diego • Detroit • New York • San Francisco • Cleveland
New Haven, Conn. • Waterville, Maine • London • Munich

LIBRARY OF CONGRESS CATALOGING-IN-PUBLICATION DATA
Werewolves / Angela Cybulski, book editor.
p. cm. — (Fact or fiction)
Includes bibliographical references and index.
ISBN 0-7377-2279-7 (pbk. : alk. paper) — ISBN 0-7377-2278-9 (alk. paper)
1. Werewolves. I. Cybulski, Angela. II. Fact or fiction (Greenhaven Press)
GR830.W4W46   2004
398'.469—dc22   2003057962

Printed in the United States of America

Contents

Foreword

"There are more things in heaven and earth, Horatio, than are dreamt of in your philosophy."
—William Shakespeare, *Hamlet*

"Extraordinary claims require extraordinary evidence."
—Carl Sagan, *The Demon-Haunted World*

Almost every one of us has experienced something that we thought seemed mysterious and unexplainable. For example, have you ever known that someone was going to call you just before the phone rang? Or perhaps you have had a dream about something that later came true. Some people think these occurrences are signs of the paranormal. Others explain them as merely coincidence.

As the examples above show, mysteries of the paranormal ("beyond the normal") are common. For example, most towns have at least one place where inhabitants believe ghosts live. People report seeing strange lights in the sky that they believe are the spaceships of visitors from other planets. And scientists have been working for decades to discover the truth about sightings of mysterious creatures like Bigfoot and the Loch Ness monster.

There are also mysteries of magic and miracles. The two often share a connection. Many forms of magical belief are tied to religious belief. For example, many of the rituals and beliefs of the voodoo religion are viewed by outsiders as magical practices. These include such things as the alleged Haitian voodoo practice of turning people into zombies (the walking dead).

There are mysteries of history—events and places that have been recorded in history but that we still have questions about today. For example, was the great King Arthur a real king or merely a legend? How, exactly, were the pyramids built? Historians continue to seek the answers to these questions.

Then, of course, there are mysteries of science. One such mystery is how humanity began. Although most scientists agree that it was through the long, slow process of evolution, not all scientists agree that indisputable proof has been found.

Subjects like these are fascinating, in part because we do not know the whole truth about them. They are mysteries. And they are controversial—people hold very strong and opposing views about them.

How we go about sifting through information on such topics is the subject of every book in the Greenhaven Press series Fact or Fiction? Each anthology includes articles that present the main ideas favoring and challenging a given topic. The editor collects such material from a variety of sources, including scientific research, eyewitness accounts, and government reports. In addition, a final chapter gives readers tools to analyze the articles they read. With these tools, readers can sift through the information presented in the articles by applying the methods of hypothetical reasoning. Examining these topics in this way adds a unique aspect to the Fact or Fiction? series. Hypothetical reasoning can be applied to any topic to allow a reader to become more analytical about the material he or she encounters. While such reasoning may not solve the mystery of who is right or who is wrong, it can help the reader separate valid from invalid evidence relating to all topics and can be especially helpful in analyzing material where people disagree.

Introduction

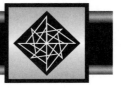

"Many a man who is pure in heart, and says his prayers by night, may become a wolf when the wolfsbane blooms and the moon shines bright."

—Ancient gypsy proverb

The dark night is lit only by the full white moon. A man walks alone on a deserted wooded path, heart racing, fearful of the change he feels coming over him. Suddenly he stops and looks down at his hands. The bones begin to crack and move, growing larger as the fingers slowly extend into claws. Hair begins to cover his body as his face contorts into the fearsome visage of a wolf. With sharp teeth bared, the werewolf's transformation is complete. His howl pierces the dark night as his hunt begins.

The image of the werewolf as a man-beast transformed by an untamed wildness that drives it to hunt, kill, and feast on innocent human blood is familiar to many people. The mystery of the werewolf has existed in cultures throughout the world for thousands of years. Dictionaries broadly define the werewolf as a human who possesses the capability to transform into a wolf in both appearance and appetite. This transformation from human into wolf can be either temporary or permanent and can occur in a variety of ways, including supernatural influences, witchcraft, or voluntary participation. Prior to the seventeenth century, it was commonly believed that individuals suspected of being werewolves had been cursed by a witch, had themselves been bitten by a werewolf, or had sold their souls to the devil to become werewolves as his minions on Earth.

The image people most commonly associate with the werewolf arose before the twelfth century based on eyewitness sightings and cultural beliefs, perhaps as a way to explain what otherwise appeared to be unexplainable. People claimed to have seen and heard strange things in the night. Missing townspeople showed up mangled or murdered. The whereabouts of suspicious individuals were unaccounted for until they later appeared with telling marks on their bodies, indicating they had been involved in some violent struggle. Individuals arrested and tried as werewolves were labeled *lycanthrope* and *werewolf*.

The wealth of eyewitness accounts and the testimonials given by those accused of being werewolves illustrate that the early encounters people had with these creatures provided a range of shared experiences that allowed for the emergence of a widely accepted, if general, definition of the werewolf. This definition focuses largely on the concept of transformation. The changes effected by transformation are fundamental, changing the person or thing to the core. In discussions of the werewolf, transformation emphasizes the idea that a human being can actually become a wolf with a wolf's form and appearance, behaviors, and desires.

It is easy for twenty-first century minds to look at the belief in a human's ability to transform as simple superstitious imaginings of folk belief. Still, although many people believe the werewolf to be a figure of superstition and folklore, others firmly believe the werewolf is not merely a creature of the imagination. They argue that a real transformation of human into beast can and does occur in a variety of ways and for a variety of reasons. To solve the mystery of the werewolf, one must first examine the mystery of transformation that lies at the heart of the creature's history.

Throughout this discussion, as well as in many of the essays included in this book, the words *lycanthrope* and *were-*

wolf will be used interchangeably when talking about were-wolves. Interestingly, these terms are used interchangeably regardless of the various arguments the authors offer on werewolves. Translated, both words mean literally the same thing, either "wolf-man" or "man-wolf." Yet, as we shall see, whereas the werewolf is typically regarded as fiction, the lycanthrope exists in fact. It is the lycanthrope and his or her relationship to a rare, but very real, mental disorder that is perhaps one key to understanding the mystery of transformation as it relates to werewolves.

Prior to the twelfth century the word *lycanthrope* was most often used to describe individuals experiencing a mental delusion (lycanthropia) in which they believed they had become wolves. According to Richard Noll, a psychiatric researcher who has done studies on the history of the werewolf in psychiatric medicine, lycanthropy is an "ancient affliction." He notes that "medical descriptions of a mental disorder [resembling it] date back at least to [A.D. 161]." The main characteristic of the disorder is "the notion of a human taking the form of a wolf and then literally behaving like one."[1] Psychologists argue that since the lycanthrope's delusion causes the transformation to take place in his or her own mind, no real transformation occurs; however, this does not necessarily mean that no visible change can be seen in the person suffering from lycanthropy. In keeping with the definition of transformation, a marked change in appearance and in the very nature of the lycanthrope takes place within the individual while in this delusional state. These physical and behavioral changes have been observed and documented by psychologists in clinical settings.

For nearly as long as werewolves have been sighted, lycanthropy has been known to exist. As a result, throughout history the term *lycanthrope* was used interchangeably with the term *werewolf* to describe those individuals thought to transform by the light of the moon into a wild beast, rampaging through the countryside killing innocent villagers, and committing other violent crimes. But this parallel existence between the two terms raises a challenging and important question: If a mental disorder exists in which a human believes himself or herself to be, and behaves as if he or she is, a werewolf, can it be argued that werewolves do in fact exist?

Transformation: The Missing Link

Over time, the basic "fact" of the clinically defined lycanthrope has merged with the presumed "fiction" of the werewolf. Richard Noll makes this point and attempts to articulate a distinction between the terms *lycanthrope* and *werewolf*:

> In English, the words lycanthrope and werewolf are often used interchangeably. . . . As is true of vampirism, lycanthropy is likewise both a clinical and a legendary phenomenon. However, over the centuries a certain convention has developed in the English language about the use of the words lycanthropy and werewolfism, or lycanthropes and werewolves. The word lycanthropy is generally used in discussions of the clinical nature of this phenomenon, whereas in the area of folklore or myths and legends involving the actual physical shape-shifting of an individual, it is more likely that werewolves will be discussed.[2]

Mental Illness and Transformation

Once lycanthropy is diagnosed for individuals claiming to transform from human into wolf, various other psychiatric diagnoses come into play as a way to explain the delusional behaviors of the lycanthrope. According to Noll, a diagnosis of "bipolar disorder is most common," but others include schizophrenia, delusional depression, major depression, borderline personality disorder, and multiple personality disorder. He goes on to suggest that "the transformation of human into animal may be analogous to the 'switching' process observed in persons with multiple personality disorder in which the personality in executive control of the body is replaced by another [personality that could be] . . . nonhuman."[3] This seems to suggest that the individual suffering from lycanthropy or another disorder is indeed capable of achieving transformation, at least within the patient's own mind.

From Human to Inhuman: The Serial Killer as Werewolf

Elliot O'Donnell, a ghost hunter and expert on the paranormal who came to believe in the existence of werewolves based on his personal experiences and research, argues that "there is no conclusive evidence that the people who claimed to be werewolves were shams."[4]

Is it possible that individuals *choose* to move from the human realm to the inhuman, and *choose* to leave the life of civility for the life of the animal? Brad Steiger, whose work appears in this volume, argues strongly that contemporary serial killers meet the defining requirements for werewolves. Steiger's position is strengthened by the fact that, in the early days of Germanic languages, the Old English word for werewolf was also used for what is now termed a serial killer. According to the *Wikipedia*, an online encyclopedia, the serial killer does indeed possess the power "to undergo transformation into an animal."[5] Speaking directly to this point, Noll explains that "because so many persons were called werewolves who committed atrocities during the Middle Ages and the Renaissance (the equivalent of our modern-day serial killers, mass murderers . . .) this term [*werewolf*] is still commonly used to refer to these sadistic criminals as well."[6] Pursuing Steiger's line of thinking, it might be argued that modern-day serial killers could suffer from lycanthropy of some form. This argument could also be made as one way of explaining eyewitness accounts of werewolves throughout history. What if the individual suffering under the delusions of lycanthropy, but who has not yet been diagnosed, commits a crime like that which was traditionally believed to have been committed by werewolves? This idea is not entirely impossible; however, lycanthropy as a mental disorder is generally acknowledged to be rare. Serial killers, on the other hand, are less so. It is perhaps going too far to suggest that all werewolf sightings can be explained as incidents of serial killers who suffered from lycanthropy, though this explanation may serve for some. Even if incidents of lycanthropy could explain some eyewitness sightings, the physical transformation that witnesses claim to see is still problematic.

Eyewitness accounts included in this volume describe actual physical changes in the appearances of individuals diagnosed with lycanthropy. This is echoed in the historical discussion of the lycanthrope found in the *Wikipedia*, which points out that "the transformation may be voluntary or involuntary, temporary or permanent, the weranimal may be the man himself metamorphosed, it may be his double whose activity leaves the real man to all appearance unchanged."[7] It might be argued that the physical transformation that an apparently mild-mannered person undergoes in the rage of murder warrants closer examination. Although hair may not sprout and fangs and nails may not grow longer, some sort of an inner transformation takes place in the appearance of the person who kills. Even Noll acknowledges that "those who refuse to obey the impulses of the greater society may choose to act out the impulses of animals: to rape, to murder, to mutilate, to cannibalize."[8] The killer is indeed a person who changes from human to beast. Perhaps there are those, whether they are called werewolves or lycanthropes, who choose to become such, to give in to their lust for blood and violence, and to live enslaved to their animal impulses.

Our Werewolves, Ourselves

Paraphrasing the work of Carl Jung, a noted psychoanalyst and pioneer of dream study who specialized in analyzing the ways in which the dark side of the human conscious/unconscious mind play out in human behavior, Noll offers the alternative suggestion that the werewolf might be a person's shadow self. As such, the creature represents the dark animal instincts society has taught us to suppress in favor of a more civilized self, but often at the expense of our emotional health. Although these tendencies are suppressed, they do not cease to exist, which means that we all possess something of the beast within ourselves. These tendencies then surface in ways that are usually socially unacceptable and may often be seen as inhuman. According to Jung, "the shadow is the primitive who is still alive and active in civilized man and our civilized reason means nothing to him."[9] Perhaps the "delusion" the lycanthrope suffers under is a term used by psychiatrists to explain a phenomenon for which we ultimately have no explanation—similar to what happened hundreds of years ago when townspeople were forced to come up with a name for the things they had seen but could not explain—unless the explanation is that werewolves do exist in some form, even in the primal, unconscious minds of humans.

If transformation can and does occur in human beings, it would seem to legitimatize the existence of the werewolf and suggest that, far from being a fiction, the werewolf can and does exist in our world. Although they allude to magical acts, earlier definitions of the werewolf did not specify how the transformation manifested other than to offer the possibility that the entire werewolf experience is based in delusion. The argument can be made that the delusion itself results in an actual transformation of both mind and body in a cause-and-effect relationship. Certainly no individual, whether diagnosed as a lycanthrope or not, would think and behave as a werewolf or act out the animalistic tendencies of the serial killer unless some transformation from human into beast had occurred. Indeed, the ability of the human to either voluntarily or involuntarily adopt the behavior and characteristics of a beast is remarkable. This ability, and the characteristics that result, has been observed not only by psychologists in clinical settings but also has been recorded in eyewitness accounts of werewolves throughout history. If one of the main arguments against the existence of werewolves is that a human being cannot physically transform into an animal, the fact that humans exhibit these animalistic behaviors and tendencies with a resulting physical change is strong evidence against it.

Meeting the Werewolf

If the werewolf, or lycanthrope, can be characterized as the beast within, then the mystery of transformation might be as simple as understanding the ways in which the beast inside breaks free to show itself through certain behaviors and characteristics. Richard Noll points out that "throughout history, the legend of the lycanthrope or werewolf has symbolized the dual nature of humankind. . . . The primal, bestial side of the human animal is in evidence in the darker urges within us all."[10] Not surprisingly, the "darker urges" of lycanthropes and werewolves are very similar, indicating some basic truths about the mystery of the werewolf and the reality of human transformation.

The Question Remains

Lycanthropes believe themselves to be werewolves and, as the selections in this book will show, an acute transformation from human into beast appears to occur. This same type of transformation is echoed repeatedly in other essays through detailed eyewitness accounts, cases of demonic possession, and the behaviors and aspects of serial killers. But it is unfair and unreasonable to assert that all individuals suspected of being werewolves are lycanthropes. Ultimately, there is no easy solution to the mystery of the werewolf. Although this book sets up arguments on two opposing sides of the issue, all of the arguments have at their core the concept of human transformation. Without this key element, the werewolf as we commonly define it would cease to exist. The reality of transformation exists above and beyond any assertion that werewolves are either fact or fiction. A clear and definitive answer on the key point of transformation might solve the entire mystery.

It is one goal of this book to provide reliable and accurate evidence to assist in thinking about and perhaps solving the mystery of whether werewolves exist in our world. To that end, this book considers examples of what are traditionally believed to be werewolves as well as clinical examples of lycanthropes. Admittedly, this complicates thinking about the mystery since the reader is forced to try to differentiate between two words that share a common history, meaning, behaviors and characteristics, as well as sharing the most important common element of transformation. Using the concept of transformation as a way to distinguish between the werewolf and the lycanthrope sets up a particular challenge for the reader, who must set aside his or her preconceived notions and approach the mystery of werewolves with the intent of explaining what appears to be unexplainable. Although this presents the reader with the possibility of creating a new understanding of the werewolf, it will also stretch the boundaries of reason, demonstrating how essential the careful and critical evaluation of all perspectives, viewpoints, and evidence (or, in some cases, the lack of it) is in attempting to determine and convey the truth behind any argument.

Notes

1. Richard Noll, ed., *Vampires, Werewolves, and Demons: Twentieth Century Reports in the Psychiatric Literature*. New York: Bruner/Mazel, 1996, pp. 83, 84.
2. Noll, *Vampires, Werewolves, and Demons*, p. 93.
3. Noll, *Vampires, Werewolves, and Demons*, p. 90.
4. Quoted in Daniel Farson, *The Supernatural: Vampires, Zombies, and Monster Men*. London: Aldus Books, 1975, p. 53.
5. *Wikipedia*, "Lycanthropy." www.wikipedia.org.
6. Noll, *Vampires, Werewolves, and Demons*, p. 85.
7. *Wikipedia*, "Lycanthropy in History." www.wikipedia.org.
8. Noll, *Vampires, Werewolves, and Demons*, p. 92.
9. Quoted in Noll, *Vampires, Werewolves, and Demons*, pp. 84–85.
10. Noll, *Vampires, Werewolves, and Demons*, p. 92.

Chapter 1

Fact or Fiction?

The Mark of the Beast: Arguments for the Existence of Werewolves

The Werewolf in France: Eyewitness Accounts and Personal Testimonies

Sabine Baring-Gould

Born into a poor family in England in 1834, Sabine Baring-Gould could speak five languages by the time he was fifteen. His giftedness and obvious intellect enabled him to pursue an education at both the prestigious King's College at Cambridge University. Baring-Gould would eventually become a well-known theologian, folklorist, and prolific writer during the nineteenth century. He is remembered for his unique and well-researched study on werewolves, first published in 1865, from which the following essay is taken.

Baring-Gould's *The Book of Werewolves* was published at a time when belief in the existence of werewolves was strong, with eyewitness sightings prevalent throughout Europe.

Sabine Baring-Gould, "A Chapter of Horrors," *The Book of Werewolves*. London: Smith, Elder, and Co., 1865.

Interestingly, the sixteenth and seventeenth centuries in France saw the numbers of werewolf sightings raised to epidemic proportions; it is this phenomenon that Baring-Gould explores here. Although he generally regarded the werewolf as a figure of superstition, Baring-Gould found he was unable to adequately explain the terror and mayhem caused by the wolf figures in these eyewitness accounts and personal testimonies. From a distance, it might be easy to dismiss these events as simple superstition or the delusional ramblings of madmen. However, not even Baring-Gould, a noted skeptic and scholar, was willing to make that argument an absolute in the end. The lack of a logical explanation for these events is an indication that more serious consideration on the existence of werewolves is needed.

[Editor's Note: The werewolf, also called the loup-garou, has a long and infamous history in France. The first account in this essay tells the story of Pierre Bourgot and Michel Verdung, two of the most violent werewolves ever captured. Baring-Gould sets their story in the context of a court hearing, which is appropriate since the Bourgot-Verdung case is one of the best documented in French legal history.]

In December, 1521, the Inquisitor-General for the diocese of Besançon [a province in France], Boin by name, heard a case of a sufficiently terrible nature to produce a profound sensation of alarm in the neighbourhood. Two men were under accusation of witchcraft and cannibalism. Their names were Pierre Bourgot, or Peter the Great, as the people had nicknamed him from his stature, and Michel Verdung. Peter had not been long under trial, before he volunteered a full confession of his crimes. It amounted to this:—

A Deal with the Devil

About nineteen years before, on the occasion of a New Year's market at Poligny, a terrible storm had broken over the country, and among other mischiefs done by it, was the scattering of Pierre's flock. "In vain," said the prisoner, "did I labour, in company with other peasants, to find the sheep and bring them together. I went everywhere in search of them.

"Then there rode up three black horsemen, and the last said to me: 'Whither away? you seem to be in trouble?'

"I related to him my misfortune with my flock. He bade me pluck up my spirits, and promised that his master would henceforth take charge of and protect my flock, if I would only rely upon him. He told me, as well, that I should find my strayed sheep very shortly, and he promised to provide me with money. We agreed to meet again in four or five days. My flock I soon found collected together. At my second meeting I learned of the stranger that he was a servant of the devil. . . .

"I fell on my knees and gave in my allegiance to Satan. I remained in the service of the devil for two years . . . according to the desire of my master, whose name I afterwards learned was Moyset.

"All anxiety about my flock was removed, for the devil had undertaken to protect it and to keep off the wolves.

"This freedom from care, however, made me begin to tire of the devil's service, and I recommenced my attendance at church, till I was brought back into obedience to the evil one by Michel Verdung, when I renewed my compact on the understanding that I should be supplied with money.

The Metamorphosis: Man into Wolf

"In a wood near Chastel Charnon we met with many others whom I did not recognize; we danced, and each had in his or her hand a green taper with a blue flame. Still under the delusion that I should obtain money, Michel [Verdung] persuaded me to move with the greatest celerity, and in order to do this, after I had stripped myself, he smeared me with a salve, and I believed myself then to be transformed into a wolf. I was at first somewhat horrified at my four wolf's feet, and the fur with which I was covered all at once, but I found that I could now travel with the speed of the wind. This could not have taken place without the help of our powerful master, who was present during our excursion, though I did not perceive him till I had recovered my human form. Michel did the same as myself.

"When we had been one or two hours in this condition of metamorphosis, Michel smeared us again, and quick as thought we resumed our human forms. The salve was given us by our masters; to me it was given by Moyset, to Michel by his own master, Guillemin."

Pierre declared that he felt no exhaustion after his excursions, though the judge inquired particularly whether he felt that prostration [total weakness or exhaustion] after his unusual exertion, of which witches usually complained. Indeed the exhaustion consequent on a were-wolf raid was so great that the lycanthropist was often confined to his bed for days, and could hardly move hand or foot. . . .

Crimes and Horror

In one of his were-wolf runs, Pierre fell upon a boy of six or seven years old, with his teeth, intending to rend and devour him, but the lad screamed so loud that he was obliged to beat a retreat to his clothes, and smear himself again, in order to recover his form and escape detection. He and Michel, however, one day tore to pieces a woman as she was gathering peas; and a M. de Chusnée, who came to her rescue, was attacked by them and killed.

On another occasion they fell upon a little girl of four years old, and ate her up, with the exception of one arm. Michel thought the flesh most delicious.

Another girl was strangled by them, and her blood lapped up. Of a third they ate merely a portion of the stomach. One evening at dusk, Pierre leaped over a garden wall, and came upon a little maiden of nine years old, engaged upon the weeding of the garden beds. She fell on her knees and entreated Pierre to spare her; but he snapped the neck, and left her a corpse, lying among her flowers. On this occasion he does not seem to have been in his wolf's shape. He fell upon a goat which he found in the field of Pierre Lerugen, and bit it in the throat, but he killed it with a knife.

Michel was transformed in his clothes into a wolf, but Pierre was obliged to strip, and the metamorphosis could not take place with him unless he were stark naked.

He was unable to account for the manner in which the hair vanished when he recovered his natural condition.

The Infamous Werewolf, Gilles Garnier

[Editor's Note: In this excerpt, Baring-Gould describes the mysterious series of events that led to the capture of the werewolf Gilles Garnier, also known as the Hermit of St. Bonnot. Garnier's crimes occurred some fifty years after those of Bourgot and Verdung. This werewolf killed many people before being captured.]

In a retired spot near Amanges, half shrouded in trees, stood a small hovel of the rudest construction; its roof was of turf, and its walls were blotched with lichen. The garden to this cot was run to waste, and the fence round it broken through. As the hovel was far from any road, and was only reached by a path over moorland and through forest, it was seldom visited, and the couple who lived in it were not such as would make many friends. The man, Gilles Garnier, was a sombre, ill-looking fellow, who walked in a stooping attitude, and whose pale face, livid complexion, and deep-set eyes under a pair of coarse and bushy brows, which met across the forehead, were sufficient to repel any one from seeking his acquaintance. Gilles seldom spoke, and when he did it was in the broadest patois of his country. His long grey beard and retiring habits procured for him the name of the Hermit of St. Bonnot, though no one for a moment attributed to him any extraordinary amount of sanctity.

The hermit does not seem to have been suspected for some time, but one day, as some of the peasants of Chastenoy were returning home from their work, through the forest, the screams of a child and the deep baying of a wolf, attracted their notice, and on running in the direction whence the cries sounded, they found a little girl defending herself against a monstrous creature, which was attacking her tooth and nail, and had already wounded her severely in five places. As the peasants came up, the creature fled on all fours into the gloom of the thicket; it was so dark that it could not be identified with certainty, and whilst some affirmed that it was a wolf, others thought they had recognized the features of the hermit. This took place on the 8th November.

On the 14th a little boy of ten years old was missing, who had been last seen at a short distance from the gates of Dôle.

The hermit of S. Bonnot was now seized and brought to trial at Dôle, when the following evidence was extracted from him and his wife, and substantiated in many particulars by witnesses.

On the last day of Michaelmas, under the form of a wolf, at a mile from Dôle, in the farm of Gorge, a vineyard belonging to Chastenoy, near the wood of La Serre, Gilles Garnier had attacked a little maiden of ten or twelve years old, and had slain her with his teeth and claws; he had then drawn her into the wood, stripped her, gnawed the flesh from her legs and arms, and had enjoyed his meal so much, that, inspired with conjugal affection, he had brought some of the flesh home for his wife Apolline.

Eight days after the feast of All Saints, again in the form of a were-wolf, he had seized another girl, near the meadow land of La Pouppe, on the territory of Athume and Chastenoy, and was on the point of slaying and devouring her, when three persons came up, and he was compelled to escape. On the fourteenth day after All Saints, also as a wolf, he had attacked a boy of ten years old, a mile from Dôle, between Gredisans and Menoté, and had strangled him. On that occasion he had eaten all the flesh off his legs and arms, and had also devoured a great part of the belly; one of the legs he had rent completely from the trunk with his fangs.

On the Friday before the last feast of S. Bartholomew, he had seized a boy of twelve or thirteen, under a large pear-tree near the wood of the village Perrouze, and had drawn him into the thicket and killed him, intending to eat him as he had eaten the other children, but the approach of men hindered him from fulfilling his intention. The boy was, however, quite dead, and the men who came up declared that Gilles appeared as a man and not as a wolf. The hermit of S. Bonnot was sentenced to be dragged to the place of public execution, and there to be burned alive, a sentence which was rigorously carried out.

In this instance the poor maniac fully believed that actual transformation into a wolf took place; he was apparently perfectly reasonable on other points, and quite conscious of the acts he had committed.

We come now to a more remarkable circumstance, the affliction of a whole family with the same form of insanity. Our information is derived from [Henri] Boguet's *Discours des Sorciers*, 1603–1610.

Pernette Gandillon was a poor girl in the Jura, who in

1598 ran about the country on all fours, in the belief that she was a wolf. One day as she was ranging the country in a fit of lycanthropic madness, she came upon two children who were plucking wild strawberries. Filled with a sudden passion for blood, she flew at the little girl and would have brought her down, had not her brother, a lad of four years old, defended her lustily with a knife. Pernette, however, wrenched the weapon from his tiny hand, flung him down and gashed his throat, so that he died of the wound. Pernette was torn to pieces by the people in their rage and horror.

Directly after, Pierre, the brother of Pernette Gandillon, was accused of witchcraft. He was charged with having led children to the sabbath [or sabbat, a midnight assembly of witches and sorcerers gathered to perform magic rites], having made hail, and having run about the country in the form of a wolf. The transformation was effected by means of a salve which he had received from the devil. He had on one occasion assumed the form of a hare, but usually he appeared as a wolf, and his skin became covered with shaggy grey hair. He readily acknowledged that the charges brought against him were well founded, and he allowed that he had, during the period of his transformation, fallen on, and devoured, both beasts and human beings. When he desired to recover his true form, he rolled himself in the dewy grass. His son Georges asserted that he had also been anointed with the salve, and had gone to the sabbath in the shape of a wolf. According to his own testimony, he had fallen upon two goats in one of his expeditions.

One Maundy-Thursday [the Thursday before Easter Sunday] night he had lain for three hours in his bed in a cataleptic state, and at the end of that time had sprung out of bed. During this period he had been in the form of a wolf to the witches' sabbath.

His sister Antoinnette confessed that she had made hail,

and that she had sold herself to the devil, who had appeared to her in the shape of a black he-goat. She had been to the sabbath on several occasions.

Pierre and Georges in prison behaved as maniacs, running on all fours about their cells and howling dismally. Their faces, arms, and legs were frightfully scarred with the wounds they had received from dogs when they had been on their raids. Boguet accounts for the transformation not taking place, by the fact of their not having the necessary salves by them.

All three, Pierre, Georges, and Antoinnette, were hung and burned.

Eyewitness Accounts of British Werewolves

Elliott O'Donnell

Elliott O'Donnell is the noted author of many books on the occult, supernatural, and related mysterious phenomena. He was born in England in 1872 and claimed to have had several experiences with the paranormal during his early years. These experiences, coupled with the wealth of evidence he gathered through years of research, solidified O'Donnell's strong personal belief in ghosts and other unexplainable phenomena. In addition to his writings on hauntings and his chronicling of eyewitness accounts of ghostly sightings, O'Donnell became well known in his later life as a ghost hunter. From his experiences researching and interviewing eyewitnesses, O'Donnell wrote his book *Werewolves*, which was published in 1912 and from which the following accounts are taken.

This piece is significant as an argument for the existence of werewolves on several levels. O'Donnell interviews aver-

Elliott O'Donnell, *Werewolves*. London: Methun and Co. Ltd., 1912.

age citizens who see things they cannot explain. They have nothing to gain by making up these accounts, and the earnestness with which their stories are told gives them a feeling of credibility. In addition, all of the eyewitnesses' descriptions of werewolves are alarmingly similar. The fact that none of the eyewitnesses knows the others gives the obvious parallels in their accounts greater importance. Finally, each of these eyewitnesses clearly saw something that he or she is unable to explain by any conventional means. O'Donnell makes it clear that each individual makes a conscious and rational effort to explore possible explanations for what he or she saw. O'Donnell concludes that, based on their individual experiences, werewolves appear to exist in Great Britain.

In my investigations of haunted houses and my psychical research work generally, I have met people who have informed me they have seen phantasms [a phantom, or apparition, with no physical being], in shape half human and half beast, that might well be the earth-bound spirits of werwolves.

The Werwolf at the Train Station

A Miss St. Denis told me she was once staying on a farm, in Merlonethshire, where she witnessed a phenomenon of this class. The farm, though some distance from the village, was not far off the railway station, a very diminutive affair, with only one platform and a mere box that served as a waiting-room and bookingoffice combined. It was, moreover, one of those stations where the separate duties of station-master, porter, booking-clerk, and ticket-collector are performed by one and the same person, and where the signal always appears to be down. As the platform commanded the only paintable view in the neighbourhood, Miss St. Denis often used to resort there with her sketch-book. On one occasion she had stayed rather later than usual, and on rising hurriedly from her campstool saw, to her surprise, a figure which she took to be that of a man, sitting on a truck a few yards distant, peering at her. I say to her surprise, because, excepting on the rare occasion of a train arriving, she had never seen anyone at the station beside the station-master, and in the evening the platform was invariably deserted. The loneliness of the place was for the first time brought forcibly home to her. The station-master's tiny house was at least some hundred yards away, and beyond that there was not another habitation nearer than the farm. . . . The darkness had come on very rapidly, and was especially concentrated, so it seemed to her, round the spot where she sat, and she could make nothing out of the silent figure on the truck, save that it had unpleasantly bright eyes and there was something queer about it. She coughed to see if that would have any effect, and as it had none she coughed again. Then she spoke and said, "Can you tell me the time, please?" But there was no reply, and the figure still sat there staring at her. Then she grew uneasy and, packing up her things, walked out of the station, trying her best to look as if nothing had occurred. She glanced over her shoulder; the figure was following her. Quickening her pace, she assumed a jaunty air and whistled, and turning round again, saw the strange figure still coming after her. The road would soon be at its worst stage of loneliness, and, owing to the cliffs on either side of it, almost pitch dark. Indeed, the spot positively invited murder, and she might shriek herself hoarse without the remotest chance of making herself heard. To go on with this outre [bizarre] figure so unmistakably and persistently stalking her, was out of the question. Screwing up courage, she swung round, and raising herself to her full height, cried: "What do you want? How dare you?"—She got no further, for a sudden spurt of dying sunlight, playing over the figure, showed her it was nothing human, nothing she had ever conceived possible. It was a nude grey thing, not unlike a man in body, but with a wolf's head. As it sprang forward, its light eyes ablaze with ferocity, she instinctively felt in her pocket, whipped out a pocket flash-light, and pressed the button. The effect was magical, the creature shrank back, and putting two paw-like hands in front of its face to protect its eyes, faded into nothingness.

She subsequently made inquiries, but could learn nothing beyond the fact that in one of the quarries close to the place where the phantasm had vanished, some curious bones, partly human and partly animal, had been unearthed, and that the locality was always shunned after dusk. Miss St. Denis thought as I did, that what she had seen might very well have been the earth-bound spirit of a werwolf.

Country Werwolves Howling at the Moon

The case of another haunting of this nature was related to me last year [exact date undertain; refers to time of author's research in the early nineteenth century, prior to 1912]. A young married couple of the name of Anderson, having acquired, through the death of a relative, a snug fortune, resolved to retire from business and spend the rest of their lives in indolence and ease. Being fond of the country, they bought some land in Cumberland, at the foot of some hills, far away from any town, and built on it a large two-storied villa.

They soon, however, began to experience trouble with their servants, who left them on the pretext that the place was lonely, and that they could not put up with the noises that they heard at night. The Andersons ridiculed their servants, but when their children remarked on the same thing they viewed the matter more seriously. "What are the noises like?" they inquired. "Wild animals," Willie, the eldest child, replied. "They come howling round the window at night and we hear their feet patter along the passage and stop at our door." Much mystified, Mr. and Mrs. Anderson decided to sit up with the children and listen. They did so, and between two and three in the morning were much startled by a noise that sounded like the growling of a wolf—Mr. Anderson had heard wolves in Canada—immediately beneath the window. Throwing open the window, he peered out; the moon was fully up and every stick and stone was plainly discernible; but there was now no sound and no sign of any animal. When he had closed the window the growling at once recommenced, yet when he looked again nothing was to be seen. After a while the growling ceased, and they heard the front door, which they had locked before coming upstairs, open, and the footsteps of some big, soft-footed animal ascend the stairs. Mr. Anderson waited till the steps were just outside the room and then flung open the door, but the light from his acetylene [gas] lamp revealed a passage full of moonbeams—nothing else.

He and his wife were now thoroughly mystified. In the morning they explored the grounds, but could find no trace of footmarks, nothing to indicate the nature of their visitant. It was now close on Christmas, and as the noises had not been heard for some time, it was hoped that the disturbances would not occur again. . . .

A Frightening Reappearance

[On Christmas Eve] their father, elaborately clad as Santa Claus, and staggering, in the orthodox fashion, beneath a load of presents, shuffled softly down the passage leading to their room. The snow had ceased falling, the moon was out, and the passage flooded with a soft, phosphorescent glow that threw into strong relief every minute object. Mr. Anderson had got half-way along it when on his ears there suddenly fell a faint sound of yelping! His whole frame thrilled and his mind reverted to the scenes of his youth—to the prairies in the far-off West, where, over and over again, he had heard these sounds, and his faithful Winchester repeater had stood him in good service. Again the yelping—this time nearer. Yes! it was undoubtedly a wolf; and yet there was an intonation in that yelping not altogether wolfish—something Mr. Anderson had never heard before, and which he was consequently at a loss to define. Again it rang out— much nearer this time, much more trying to the nerves, and the cold sweat of fear burst out all over him. Again—close under the wall of the house—a moaning, snarling, drawn-out cry that ended in a whine so piercing that Mr. Anderson's knees shook. One of the children, Violet Evelyn he thought, stirred in her bed and muttered: "Santa Claus! Santa Claus!" and Mr. Anderson, with a desperate effort, staggered on under his load and opened their door. The clock in the hall beneath began to strike twelve. Santa Claus, striving hard to appear jolly and genial, entered the room, and a huge grey, shadowy figure entered with him. A slipper thrown by Willie whizzed through the air, and, narrowly missing Santa Claus, fell to the ground with a clatter. There was then a deathly silence, and Violet and Horace, raising their heads, saw two strange figures standing in the centre of the room staring at one another—the one figure they at once identified by the costume. He was Santa Claus—but not the genial, rosy-cheeked Santa Claus their father had depicted. On the contrary, it was a Santa Claus with a very white face and frightened eyes—a Santa Claus that shook as if the snow and ice had given him the ague. But the other figure—what was it? Something very tall, far taller than their father, nude and grey, something like a man with the head of a wolf—a wolf with white pointed teeth and horrid, light eyes. Then they understood why it was that Santa Claus trembled; and Willie stood by the side of his bed, white and silent. It is impossible to say how long this state of things would have lasted, or what would eventually have happened, had not Mrs. Anderson, anxious to see how Santa Claus was faring, and rather wondering why he was gone so long, resolved herself to visit the children's room. As the light from her candle appeared on the threshold of the room the thing with the wolf's head vanished. . . .

An Investigation Reveals Evidence

On the following day it was proposed, and carried unanimously, that the house should be put up for sale. This was done at the earliest opportunity, and fortunately for the Andersons suitable tenants were soon found. Before leaving, however, Mr. Anderson made another and more exhaustive search of the grounds, and discovered, in a cave in the hills immediately behind the house, a number of bones. Amongst them was the skull of a wolf, and lying close beside it a human skeleton, with only the skull missing. Mr. Anderson burnt the bones, hoping that by so doing he would rid the house of its unwelcome visitor; and, as his tenants so far have not complained, he believes that the hauntings have actually ceased. . . .

A Werwolf in Rural Scotland

Here is another account of this type of haunting narrated to me some summers ago by a Mr. Warren, who at the time he saw the phenomenon was staying in the Hebrides, which part of the British Isles is probably richer than any other in spooks of all sorts.

"I was about fifteen years of age at the time," Mr. Warren said, "and had for several years been residing with my grandfather, who was an elder in the Kirk of Scotland [the

Presbyterian Church of Scotland]. He was much interested in geology, and literally filled the house with fossils from the pits and caves round where we dwelt. One morning he came home in a great state of excitement, and made me go with him to look at some ancient remains he had found at the bottom of a dried-up tarn. 'Look!' he cried, bending down and pointing at them, 'here is a human skeleton with a wolf's head. What do you make of it?' I told him I did not know, but supposed it must be some kind of monstrosity. 'It's a werwolf!' he rejoined, 'that's what it is. A werwolf! This island was once overrun with satyrs [creatures that are half man and half goat] and werwolves! Help me carry it to the house.' I did as he bid me, and we placed it on the table in the back kitchen. That evening I was left alone in the house, my grandfather and the other members of the household having gone to the kirk. For some time I amused myself reading, and then, fancying I heard a noise in the back premises, I went into the kitchen. There was no one about, and becoming convinced that it could only have been a rat that had disturbed me, I sat on the table alongside the alleged remains of the werwolf, and waited to see if the noises would recommence. I was thus waiting in a listless sort of way, my back bent, my elbows on my knees, looking at the floor and thinking of nothing in particular, when there came a loud rat, tat, tat of knuckles on the window-pane. I immediately turned in the direction of the noise and encountered, to my alarm, a dark face looking in at me. At first dim and indistinct, it became more and more complete, until it developed into a very perfectly defined head of a wolf terminating in the neck of a human being. Though greatly shocked, my first act was to look in every direction for a possible reflection—but in vain. There was no light either without or within, other than that from the setting sun—nothing that could in any way have produced an illusion. I looked at the face and marked each feature intently. It was unmistakably a wolf's face, the jaws slightly distended; the lips wreathed in a savage snarl; the teeth sharp and white; the eyes light green; the ears pointed. The expression of the face was diabolically malignant, and as it gazed straight at me my horror was as intense as my wonder. This it seemed to notice, for a look of savage exultation crept into its eyes, and it raised one hand—a slender hand, like that of a woman, though with prodigiously long and curved finger-nails—menacingly, as if about to dash in the window-pane. Remembering what my grandfather had told me about evil spirits, I crossed myself; but as this had no effect, and I really feared the thing would get at me, I ran out of the kitchen and shut and locked the door, remaining in the hall till the family returned."

Italian Werewolves: Accounts and Characteristics

Louis C. Jones

Writer and folklorist Louis C. Jones received a Guggenheim Fellowship to research the stories of werewolf sightings that had been handed down among generations of Italian American immigrants through the mid-1940s. The following excerpt is based on reports Jones collected from his Italian American students between 1940 and 1946 while teaching a folklore seminar at New York State College for Teachers. The essay relates several popular stories circulated about the werewolf in Italy, as well as detailed descriptions of werewolf behaviors and traits. Jones never asserts that werewolves exist; however, this collection of werewolf accounts representing a segment of the twentieth-century Italian American belief system has been handed down over generations and is continuing to be preserved. The continued circulation of these stories raises the possibility that, even

Louis C. Jones, "Italian Werewolves," *New York Folklore Quarterly*, vol. 6, 1950, pp. 133–38.

though the stories told took place in the "old country," the belief in these creatures has never completely vanished. Like other eyewitness accounts collected in this volume, these stories have an eerily believable quality that is enough to cast a shadow of doubt in the minds of werewolf skeptics, thus making Jones's piece worthy of inclusion here.

Just as some people are born with the evil eye, so others are cursed from birth with a tendency to turn into wolves, under certain circumstances, and go howling through the night with slavering jaws. The Folklore Archive at the Farmers' Museum contains a few accounts of the appearance of the werewolf, or *loupgarou*, among the French-Canadians who live in northern New York, but for the most part it is from Italians that the helpful information comes.[1]

A typical story is told by Mrs. Frank Roschnotti, who heard it from her aunt, who in turn heard it from her mother-in-law's father, Anthony Compatello, who was a neighbor of the man of whom this account tells.

The Christmas Curse

It was nearly a hundred years ago in St. Angelo, Italy, that a boy was born on the very stroke of twelve, Christmas Eve. But there was no rejoicing in that household, for all present knew that the child born at the moment in the year sacred to the *Bambino* [Christ child] must carry always the curse of the wolf. His family reared him gently and he grew to be a likable fellow; except for a few moments each year he was a perfectly normal person.

It was every Christmas Eve that his spell came over him. At a quarter to twelve he would start off for the church, but when he got there, he would take off his clothes and leave them on the steps. He would begin by running up and down the streets, howling into the night; he could see and feel himself change: his eyes grew blurry; his arms and hair grew long. All who knew him locked their doors, for all knew that, against his normal will and unknown to his natural self, he would kill anyone he saw.

On one occasion a friend hid in an empty barrel equipped with a long stick to which was attached a sharp pin. He hoped that he would be able to stick the werewolf in the middle of the forehead sufficiently to draw a little blood, thus curing him of his malady. But unfortunately the mad animal saw him and rolled the barrel down a hill into a deep stream, where the man was drowned.

A Fatal Mistake

When he married, the man-wolf was perfectly frank with his wife about the whole matter and gave her careful instructions for her protection on the one night in the year when he would not be himself. (Werewolves seem to be brought back by some cruel instinct to their own families.) Once he had left the house, she was not to go to sleep; she should lock the door against him and not open it under any circumstances until he knocked *three* times. For a year or two this apparently worked out satisfactorily, but one Christmas Eve she fell asleep, waking with a start to hear her husband's knock. Only half awake, she thought she had heard three knocks and opened the door to him. But she was mistaken, and her wolf-husband tore the life out of her throat.

When the spell had passed, he went to a stream of water and washed himself; as he did, the hair receded and his body took on its normal shape. Quietly he returned to the church steps and put his clothes back on. Then he went home, opening the door upon the torn and bloody corpse of his well-loved wife. He could not remember, but he knew. He did then the only thing he could to put his troubled spirit at peace: he took his own life. . . .

Characteristics of the Italian Werewolf

There is almost unanimous agreement among Italians who know of the werewolf that he is born on Christmas Eve and that it is on his birthnight anniversary that he runs wild through the streets and the woods. Occasionally one will tell you that those who are born in the full of the moon are liable to this lycanthropy, and that whenever the moon is full and it is midnight, the sickness may come over them. Usually the spell lasts but for a few hours, regardless of when it comes; only one informant insists that it comes three successive nights: Christmas Eve, Christmas night, and the night of Christmas Second Day. Always it is midnight.

There seems to be some indecision about the exact shape which the werewolf takes. In the story just told, it is implied that while his hair grew long and the inner spirit of the man became lupine, yet he was a man-shape. Very often the metamorphosis is complete: the nails grow into claws, the face becomes a snout, and the body hair turns to fur; he runs on all fours; the man has become a wolf in every respect. Some think of him as "half man, half wolf," but one and all agree to the bright, bloodshot eyes, gleaming through the night.

Curing and Killing the Werewolf

The attempt to prick the werewolf so that a few drops of blood will fall is the standard procedure for bringing one out of his fit. This need only be a minute scratch, though some insist that he must see the blood. There is disagreement as to the permanency of the cure thus affected; while one will tell you that it brings him out of his spell for that night only, others are most emphatic in insisting that the flowing of his own blood while in his wolf-shape will cure him forever. Obviously it was this hope which caused the friends to make such careful preparations for pricking the werewolf of St. Angelo. . . .

The method used by the werewolf to reassume his own shape, namely, bathing in water, is the traditional one. Sometimes his friends or family threw a bucket of water over him to hasten the process.

While some will tell you that a werewolf never dies, others insist he can be killed by the conventional silver bullet or by pricking *three* times with a needle. The trouble with this last is that it is so hard to get near enough and have time enough to do it. By the time you get to the third prick, the werewolf is gnawing at your throat. Many of the accounts speak of the danger of a werewolf killing those he attacks, and it is evident that he is fatally attracted to members of his own family.

One interesting protective device against a werewolf is to stand on the third step of any stairway, especially on the third step of a church porch. And, of course, no werewolf has any power not implicit in his wolf-shape. Once his metamorphosis has taken place, he has no supernatural powers until he shifts shape a second time.

The Story of the Bride and Groom

Another story which is frequently repeated among Sicilians and Italians concerns a bride and groom. They were happy together and whenever an opportunity arose, they would pack a little lunch and have a picnic together in the woods. One day the wife had wrapped a lunch for them in a great white napkin, and they went happily into the forest where they blissfully spread out their food and ate it. After a little while a cloud passed over the husband's spirits and he said that he was going for a little walk by himself. There were, he told her, wild dogs in those parts and he was insistent that she climb a tree before he went off, so that he would be sure she was out of harm's way. A few minutes after he had left, she heard a noise in the brush and looking down saw a wolf coming toward her with terrific speed. She watched from her perch while he pawed the ground and howled up at her; but she was increasingly afraid and in her fright she dropped the napkin she had thoughtlessly carried up the tree with her. The beast clawed at it and tore it to shreds with his teeth. After a while he went away, and a long time after that the poor, scared girl climbed down. When her husband returned to her he seemed exhausted—too tired even to listen to her terrified recital. Indeed, he went to sleep while she was telling him about it. As he slept his mouth fell open, and to her fresh horror she saw the threads of her white napkin caught between his teeth. Only a few weeks after that, the young wife died. . . .

In conclusion it ought to be noted that among the great variety of people living in New York State to whom the werewolf is a folkloristic commonplace in their native lands, it is only with the French-Canadians and Italians that the material seems to survive in this country in any profusion.

Note

1. This study is based on 36 reports collected between 1940 and 1946 by the author's students in American Folklore at the New York State College for Teachers, Albany, and now a part of the Folklore Archive, Farmers' Museum, Cooperstown. This is a segment from a longer work written under a Guggenheim Fellowship in 1946–1947.

The Werewolf Metamorphosis

Montague Summers

After retiring from the priesthood, Montague Summers spent many years as an independent scholar and author during the early twentieth century. He is primarily known for his vast research and writings on the occult, in which he explored the history of the reasons behind human belief in the supernatural, including witches, demons, vampires, and werewolves. Summers approached his studies in all of these areas from the perspective of his strong religious faith and the certain knowledge that the supernatural powers of Satan are integral to the continuing existence of these creatures in our world. In his book *The Werewolf*, from which the following essay is taken, Summers gives a summary of the extensive research of philosophers and demonologists who, throughout the centuries, have attempted to answer one central question: Assuming werewolves do exist, is the transformation physical, mental, or spiritual? How is this accomplished? So begins Summers' lengthy and complex collection of a century's worth of studies, writings, court proceedings, eyewitness accounts, and focused research on the central question surrounding this mystery. Essentially organized into two parts, the first section of the essay presents the major work of various demonologists who present evidence arguing in favor of various types of transformation. The second part summarizes three agreed-upon ways in which the transformation from man into wolf can occur. Although readers may have difficulty believing the evidence Summers amasses to support his argument, they will find it difficult to argue with the strength of faith that guides it.

When a man is metamorphosed into a wolf, or into any other animal form whatsoever it may be, is there an actual, corporeal, and material change, or else is the shape-shifting fantastical, although none the less real and substantially apparent to the man himself and to those who behold him; and if it be thus simulated and illusory how is the phenomenon accomplished?

Jean Bodin: A Case for Physical Transformation

The famous Jean Bodin [the well-known scholar, philosopher, and witch hunter] who devotes the sixth chapter of the second book of his *De la Demonomanie des Sorciers* (Paris, 1580) to a study of lycanthropy . . . gives it as his opinion that the demon can really and materially metamorphose the body of a man into that of an animal, only he cannot change and alter the human understanding. . . .

There are, it is true, other learned and weighty writers who have maintained that (under God) the Devil has power actually to change a human being corporeally into a wolf or some other animal, but it was Bodin who was universally regarded and so violently attacked as the chief exponent of this argument. His chapter is of prime importance in the history of the philosophical conceptions of lycanthropy, and demands a particular examination.

He commences by emphasizing the fact that the trans-vection [the act of moving or carrying over] of witches to the sabbat [a midnight assembly of witches and sorcerers to perform mystic rites] although sometimes fantastical, since the witch lies in a trance whilst psychically she assists at Satan's synagogue, is also oftener material, and she travels thither bodily conveyed. The Devil deludes her so that she imagines she is carried by the power of some muttered words or by the force of the sorcerers' unguent. At these orgies the demon generally appears to the assembly in the form of a huge he-goat. Sometimes he shows himself as a tall dark man. . . .

Bodin then rehearses in some detail the case of Gilles Garnier, condemned and executed for lycanthropy at Dole, 18th January, 1583, and refers to the trial of Pierre Burgot and Michel Verdun, two notorious werewolves, in 1521. He also cites the instance of the lycanthrope of Padua, as described by Job Fincel; and the coven of witches who under the form of cats met in the old haunted castle of Vernon. When some of these animals had been wounded, certain old women were found hurt in exactly the same place on their bodies. There is also the example of the woodchopper who lived in a town not far from Strasburg. Whilst hewing faggots [firewood] this man was attacked by three fierce cats. These he drove off with great difficulty, beating them back and bastooning them, where there were presently found three women of family and reputation so bruised and injured that they perforce kept their beds. All circumstances agreed beyond any shadow of doubt or incertitude. . . .

From whatever cause this shape-shifting may arise, it is

very certain by the common consent of all antiquity and all history, by the testimony of learned men, by experience and first-hand witness, that werewolfism which involves some change of form from man to animal is a very real and a very terrible thing. (It cannot, of course, take place without the exercise of black magic.) . . .

Such briefly is the tenor of Bodin's famous chapter, and there is assuredly no impossible or unsound doctrine implicated in his theory as it stands, whatever falsity may have been, and indeed actually was, read into his thesis by his enemies.

Jean de Sponde: The Perception of a Transformation

The erudite Jean de Sponde in his *Commentary upon Homer*, . . . has a very ample note upon the tenth book of the *Odyssey*, in which he discusses in detail the possibility of the transformation of the human shape to a beast, in reference to the magic of Circe. He says: "The general opinion is that the human frame cannot be metamorphosed into the animal bodies of beasts: but most hold that although there is no real shape-shifting the Devil can so cheat and deceive men's eyes that by his power they take one form, which they seem to see, to be quite another thing from what it actually is." From this he differs. The question is, whether men can be changed into animals, that is whether one body can be substantially transformed into another? If one considers carefully and weighs the extraordinary and unknown forces of nature, or if one surveys the dark dominion of Satan, such a change is not to be deemed impossible. "I believe," he frankly admits, "that in the wide circuit of this world there are so many unknown and mysterious agents, that there may be some quality which effects this metamorphosis. I am very well aware that many of my readers will deem me impious or trivial." Jean de Sponde then . . . speaks at length of noxious herbs, such as Cohobba, which grows in the isle of Haiti, and which drives men mad. Does not then this herb affect their reason? Are not those possessed by the Devil wounded, as it were, in their souls? And if a herb, and the power of evil, can have such control over the higher part of man, his reason and his immortal soul, why cannot a man's body be subject to similar disturbances? The change, although corporeal and complete, may be considered accidental, not essential. We may well believe that the Devil will employ potions and unguents, having no power in themselves, to effect such metamorphosis.

The question is can men be turned into beasts? . . . *I affirm that they can be so changed.*

Jean de Sponde then refers to the authority of Bodin. . . . He quotes various examples of werewolves, such as Gilles Garnier, Pierre Burgot, Michel Verdun, and others, cases which nobody would think of denying. That these foul warlocks were demoniac lycanthropes admits of no question, the point is how do we explain their lycanthropy.

It is sufficient for de Sponde to safeguard his position by acknowledging that a man cannot be said absolutely to be a wolf unless his soul change into the spirit of a wolf, and that is not possible. . . .

Pierre Mamor: A Case of Demonic Possession

In his eighth and ninth chapters [of *Flagellum Maleficorum*, the eminent theologian Pierre] Mamor discusses at length the glamour and diabolical illusion, and shows that men are both objectively and subjectively deceived by the demon, their senses corrupted, cheated, and tricked; the imagination clouded and betrayed. In chapter xi he treats of fascination and fantastical spells. The question of men who appear to be transformed into wolves or other animal forms arises. . . . In Mamor's judgment the werewolf is a wolf possessed by the demon, who has cast the sorcerer into a deep trance meanwhile and concealed him in some secret spot. Mamor also points out how fearful and terrible a monster is the werewolf, a hell-possessed and devil-driven wolf, two fierce relentless enemies of man joined in one body of prey.

Our author then relates a werewolf story. A peasant's wife of Lorraine to her horror saw her husband vomit up a child's arm and hand, which he had devoured when he was in a wolf's form. "I believe," says Mamor, "that this was a demoniacal illusion." None the less, he adds, Pierre de Bressuire, a most learned and pious doctor, deemed that the human body could be metamorphosed to a lupine form corporeally, "but I prefer to go no further than [Saint] Augustine, and I hold that when a werewolf rushed among the flocks and herds, tearing and ravaging, the body of the man was lying entranced in some secret chamber or retreat, whilst his spirit had entered and was energizing the form of a wolf.". . .

It is not to be denied that in the case of the demoniac werewolf there is a change, both subjective and objective, so that the warlock seems to be a wolf both to himself and also is seen as a wolf by all who observe him. . . .

Fra Spina: A Case of Witchcraft

In his *Quaestio de Strigibus* Fra Bartolomeo Spina devotes the eighth chapter to a consideration whether witches by diabolical art can turn men and women into brute beasts. He writes that although the demon cannot make material new forms, which is essentially an act of Creation, he can so confuse, commingle, and intermix already existing forms that fantastically he represents to any who behold the human form in a brute shape. Nay more, the subject of such diabolical art and working will steadfastly believe that he is become such or such an animal, and will act according to that brute nature. . . .

"It is no matter for wonder that when certain women are deluded and deceived by diabolic and fantastical agencies they exhibit the very nature, the form and likeness, the agility and feline proclivities of cats, and they are persuaded that they are cats, whilst those of their company believe them to be cats, and they in turn believe that those of their society are also cats. This is amply proven by the free confessions of such women."

An explanation of this may very well be that the demon has from certain natural elements formed an aerial body in the shape of a cat, and interposing this fantastical body between the sight of the eyes and the essential human body he thus deceives and deludes one and all.

No thinking person can deny that these witches in the form of cats suck the blood of children and overlook them, and indeed not unseldom kill them by diabolical agency. That many such delusions are wrought cannot be doubted, and the supernatural method in which this is accomplished may be ambiguous. It may be admitted that witches are themselves often mocked and tricked by the demon when they think they are actually cats, and even when they deem they are sucking the blood of some child, for as the demon impresses upon their imagination and vision the form of some animal so may he offer to their sight and taste some fluid of the colour and savour of blood. For as [Saint] Thomas allows, the Devil can entirely bemuse and cheat the senses.

At the same time it is very probable, and indeed it has often been known to happen, that witches do actually and indeed suck children's blood, which they draw either by some sharp needle or by the scratch of their long nails, or else by the aid of the Devil they pierce some vital vein, and scars are left in the tenderest parts of the child's body, whence they have sucked the hot life-blood, and the child becomes anaemic, wastes away, and dies. This cannot be gainsaid since it is proven by irrefragable [impossible to refute or dispute] testimony, and it has been demonstrated that after witches in the form of cats have been seen to attack children, blood is noticed to trickle and trill from wounds, although they may be very small, and accordingly the Devil hath been busy there.

That these cat-witches should find their way most stealthily and silkily into bedchambers, leap walls, run with exceeding nimbleness and speed, and in every way behave as grimalkins [old female cats] wont, is not at all surprising, for they accomplish these actions by the Devil's aid, who assists them lending them excessive fleetness, a swift motion impossible to natural man. Many who have seen these cat-witches have borne witness to these facts, and such circumstances are amply proven and received.

In fine, I doubt whether the whole matter has better been summed up than here. For as the Devil aids the cat-witch, this demon animal that has all the proclivities of a cat, so will he energize the werewolf, who will thus be possessed of all the savagery and fiercest instincts of a ravening wolf. . . .

Modern Perspectives: Astral Projection and Madness

It will here be interesting to consider one or two of the more modern views of lycanthropy. . . .

In *The Mysteries of Magic* Éliphas Lévi writes: "We must here speak of lycanthropy, or the nocturnal transformation of men into wolves, histories so well substantiated that sceptical science has had recourse to furious manias, and to masquerading as animals for explanations. But such hypotheses are puerile [childish], and explain nothing."

This author gives it as his opinion that werewolfery is due

to the "sidereal [astral; of or relating to the constellations] body, which is the mediator between the soul and the material organism", and largely influenced by a man's habitual thought being attached by strong sympathetic links to the heart and brain. Thus in the case of a man whose instinct is savage and sanguinary [bloodthirsty], his phantom will wander abroad in lupine form, whilst he sleeps painfully at home, dreaming he is a veritable wolf. The body being subject to nervous and magnetic influences will receive the blows and cuts dealt at the fantastical shape.

C.W. Leadbeater, in his *The Astral Plane, Its Scenery, Inhabitants and Phenomena*, offers a theosophical explanation of the many problems concerning vampires and werewolves. His view is that certain astral entities are able to materialize the "astral body" of a perfectly brutal and cruel man who has gained some knowledge of magic, and these fiends drive on this "astral body", which they mould into "the form of some wild animal, usually the wolf", to blood and maraud.

In his monograph, *The Book of Were-Wolves*, [Sabine] Baring-Gould is inclined to attribute werewolfery, the terrible truth of which he does not for a moment evade, to a species of madness, during the accesses of which the person afflicted believes himself to be a wild beast and acts like a wild beast. "In some cases this madness amounts apparently to positive possession."

Mr. Elliott O'Donnell, in his *Werewolves*, remarks that "the actual process of the metamorphosis savours of the superphysical". The werewolf is sometimes in outward form a wolf, sometimes partly wolf and partly human. This may be the result of the fact that he is "a hybrid of the material and immaterial". The opinions of those whose views of the werewolf postulate a complete denial of the supernatural need not, I think, detain us here, and are in themselves unworthy of record.

We may now proceed to inquire how this change, the shape-shifting, was effected. In the case of those who were metamorphosed involuntarily, the transformation was, of course, caused by some spell cast over them through the malignant power of a witch.

With regard to the voluntary werewolf, under whom for this consideration we may include any kind of shape-shifting. In the first place, an essential circumstance and condition is a pact, formal or tacit, with the demon. Such metamorphosis can only be wrought by black magic. . . .

How Transformation Occurs

In fine, shape-shifting may be accomplished in three ways. The first method is by a glamour caused by the demon, so that the man changed (either voluntarily or under the influence of a spell) will seem both to himself and to all who behold him to be metamorphosed into the shape of a certain animal, and although, if it be a spell which has been cast upon him, he retains his human reason he cannot exercise the power of speech. The authors of the *Malleus Maleficarum* tell us that such transmutations are "proved by authority, by reason, and by experience". . . . Henri Boguet [the author and presiding justice over many European witchcraft trials] allows another mode, for he writes: "My own opinion is that Satan sometimes leaves the witch asleep behind a bush, and himself goes and performs that which the witch has in mind to do, giving himself the appearance of a wolf; but that he so confuses the wolf's imagination that he believes he has really been a wolf and has run about and killed men and beasts. . . . And when it happens that they find themselves wounded, it is Satan who immediately transfers to them the blow which he has received in his assumed body." "When the witch is not bodily present at all," says [the famous demonologist Francesco] Guazzo, "then the Devil wounds her in that part of her absent body corresponding to the wound which he knows to have been received by the beast's body." We have here then a complete explanation of the phenomenon of repercussion, namely, that if the werewolf be wounded or maimed the witch will be found to be instantaneously wounded in numerically the same spot or maimed of the identical corresponsive limb, a piece of evidence which occurs again and again in the trials of lycanthropes. Guazzo tells us that on these occasions the demon "assumes the body of a wolf formed from the air and wrapped about him", whilst other authorities rather hold that the demon actually possesses some wolf. But whichever it be, this detail skills not. Moreover, as the learned Capuchin, Jacques d'Autun, [a theologian and demonologist,] teaches us, even if this method be employed in shape-shifting, and the sorcerer is thrown into a mesmeric trance, whilst the familiar [a spirit servant, which usually takes an animal form] prowls abroad, the consenting witch is none the less guilty of the murders and ravages wrought by the demon in lupine form, and by very force of his evil pact with hell he cannot in any whit disculpate [free from blame] himself from the shedding of blood and bestial savagery.

This method of werewolfism and metamorphosis, although infrequent, is amply proven. It does not, however, account for the immense weariness felt by the sorcerer after his animal expeditions and courses of the night. . . . By the very confessions of the witches themselves it was acknowledged that when the demon "carries his disciples through the air in this manner, he leaves them far more heavily overcome with weariness than if they had completed a rough journey afoot with the greatest urgency". Father Jacques d'Autun points out that the cases when the sorcerer is thrown into a coma, and the ravages of lycanthropy are impressed upon his imaginative faculty by the demon, so that he supposes himself as a wolf actually to have been galloping tantivy [at full speed] over hill and dale, through forest and bosky dingle [small wooded or shrubby valley] are very rare; and to attribute the decrepit lassitude of the werewolf merely to the sick fantasy of a nightmare cannot but be regarded as inconsequential and vain.

The third method by which shape-shifting may be accomplished, and that which from accumulated evidence would seem to be immeasurably the more general mode of werewolfism and other devilish transformation, cannot be better described than in the words of Guazzo: "Sometimes, in accordance with his pact, the demon surrounds a witch with an aerial effigy of a beast, each part of which fits on to the correspondent part of the witch's body, head to head, mouth to mouth, belly to belly, foot to foot, and arm to arm; but this only happens when they use certain ointments and words. . . . In this last case it is no matter for wonder if they are afterwards found with an actual wound in those parts of their human body where they were wounded when in the appearance of a beast; for the enveloping air easily yields, and the true body receives the wound."

"I maintain," says Boguet, "that for the most part it is the witch himself who runs about slaying: not that he is metamorphosed into a wolf, but that it appears to him that he is so." A little later he adds, after having reviewed the confessions of the lycanthropes at their trial: "Who now can doubt but that these witches themselves ran about and committed the acts and murders of which we have spoken? For what was the cause of the fatigue they experienced? If they had been sleeping behind some bush, how did they become fatigued? What caused the scratches on their persons, if it was not the thorns and bushes through which they ran in their pursuit of man and animals?" "They confessed also that they tired themselves with running." Clauda Jamprost, a horrible hag, old and lame, when asked how it happened that she was able to clamber over rocks and boulders in the swift midnight venery [hunt or chase], answered that she was borne along by Satan. "But this in no way renders them immune from fatigue.". . .

Man as Beast

Not without reason did the werewolf in past centuries appear as one of the most terrible and depraved of all bond-slaves of Satan. He was even whilst in human form a creature within whom the beast—and not without prevailing—struggled with the man. Masqued and clad in the shape of the most dreaded and fiercest denizen of the forest the witch came forth under cover of darkness, prowling in lonely places, to seek his prey. By the force of his diabolic pact he was enabled, owing to a ritual of horrid ointments and impious spells, to assume so cunningly the swift shaggy brute that save by his demoniac ferocity and superhuman strength none could distinguish him from the natural wolf. The werewolf loved to tear raw human flesh. He lapped the blood of his mangled victims, and with gorged reeking belly he bore the warm offal of their palpitating entrails to the sabbat to present in homage and foul sacrifice to the Monstrous Goat who sat upon the throne of worship and adoration. His appetites were depraved beyond humanity. In bestial rut he covered the fierce she-wolves amid their bosky lairs. If he were attacked and sore wounded, if a limb, a paw or ear were lopped, perforce he must regain his human shape, and he fled to some cover to conceal these fearful transformations, where man broke through the shell of beast in horrid confusion. The human body was maimed or wounded in that numerical place where the beast had been hurt. By this were his bedevilments not unseldom betrayed, he was recognized and brought to justice.

Twentieth-Century Werewolves

Brad Steiger

Writing since the 1960s, Brad Steiger has become one of the foremost authorities on UFOs and the paranormal. He is considered an expert on various psychic, spiritual, and physical aspects of human transformation. In *The Werewolf Book*, from which the following essay is taken, Steiger creates an encyclopedic history of knowledge concerning the transformation of man into beast. In this excerpt Steiger argues for the existence of werewolves, claiming a close relationship between humans and wolves that has existed since the dawn of time. His evidence demonstrates that, far from being the deranged, bloodthirsty beasts of the forests described in eyewitness accounts, there are very real modern-day werewolves who just might be the seemingly harmless man next door. Steiger claims that murderers such as Jeffrey Dahmer, Henry Lee Lucas, and Harry Gordon are, in effect, werewolves. His assertions force the reader to examine his or her own beliefs and assumptions regarding werewolves and how they are defined. Serving as a cautionary tale of the

Brad Steiger, *The Werewolf Book: The Encyclopedia of Shapeshifting Beings*. Farmington Hills, MI: Visible Ink Press, 1999. Copyright © 1999 by Brad Steiger and Sherry Hansen Steiger. Reproduced by permission.

dangers of assuming that creatures such as werewolves do not exist, Steiger's examples indicate how important it is to question our assumptions about the things we often take for granted.

One can read a frightening book about vampires or a host of other scary monsters and feel secure in the knowledge that they are merely creatures born of the dark side of human imagination seeking to define the shadow world beyond death and the awful things that go bump in the night. Werewolves, however, constitute a very different, and much more frightening, reality. Werewolves are real!

Not only do werewolves really exist, but everyone who will ever read this book has the seed of the wolf within his or her psyche. Since prehistoric times the bloodline of the wolf has blended with that of our own species, and each one of us bears the personal responsibility of honoring the noble aspects of our lupine heritage and, at the same time, keeping the savage bloodlust under control. It is to be hoped that the vast majority of those who read this book have mastered the challenge of sublimating [expressing a primitive desire in a more socially acceptable way] and channeling [controlling thoughts and actions] their lycanthropic impulses into positive and constructive outlets.

In December 1998, biologist John Allman of the California Institute of Technology stated in his new book, *Evolving Brains*, that canines and humans formed a common bond more than 140,000 years ago and evolved together in one of the most successful partnerships ever fashioned. The wolf's strength, stamina, keen sense of hearing, and extraordinary sense of smell helped humans to hunt prey and to overcome predators. Because humans (*Homo sapiens*) teamed up with wolves, they became better hunters and thus supplanted the rival species of *Homo erectus* and *Neanderthal*.

Humans and wolves even share a similar social structure. Both species employ a cooperative rearing strategy for their offspring, with both parents participating in the feeding and rearing process. In most mammals, the care of the young is left almost exclusively to the mother. Wolves practice fidelity and mate for life, thus setting an early model for the family structure that humans violate more than their canine partners. Wolf packs also have dominant members, like any tribe or community, and humans probably began the domestication process by assuming the role of the dominant wolf and achieving acquiescence from the lupine leader. In turn, wolves may have perceived humans sharing food with their pups as the act of responsible members who helped support the pack.

If, as Allman and other researchers have suggested, the human species may have greatly depended upon wolves for its continued existence, then it may be clearly understood why early humans may have modeled so much of their behavior, especially in the area of survival skills, upon the wolf. As these prehistoric "wolf men" learned over time to hunt in packs and, with the assistance of their wolf allies, to subdue much larger predators, then certain elements of lupine savagery may well have been "inherited" along with the more noble aspects of a sense of community and mutual support.

While most of us have become "domesticated" and hearken to the inner voice of conscience that has been strengthened by moral and spiritual values cultivated over centuries of civilized behavior, those individuals who have succumbed to the more vicious seed of the wolf within them walk among us today as those sadistic sex criminals who slash, tear, rip, rape, mutilate, and cannibalize their victims.

When one compares the details of the offenses charged to alleged werewolves during the witchcraft mania of the Middle Ages with the offenses attributed to such sex criminals as the Chicago Rippers, Harry Gordon, Richard Ramirez, Henry Lee Lucas, and Jeffrey Dahmer, it becomes clear that there exists a true werewolf psychosis that can cause people to believe that they are transformed into wolves or can cause them to commit cruel and vicious crimes as if they were wolves scratching, biting, and killing their prey.

While the werewolf as sex criminal constitutes a very grim reality and a serious physical threat to unsuspecting members of society who are its potential victims, the werewolf as a creature of superstition poses a psychic threat to those who may trespass beyond the boundaries of logic and reason into the dangerous and uncharted regions of the supernatural. The werewolf of tradition is the deliberate creation of a human who, motivated by a desire for power or revenge, has sought to release the beast within and accomplish the transformation of human into wolf. Therefore, one becomes a werewolf through a self-willed and carefully structured magical quest to achieve a metamorphosis into wolf. In those instances wherein one has become a werewolf against his or her will, it is because a powerful and evil sorcerer has created the terrible transformation through the malignant energy of a curse. . . .

The wild hunts with the wolf packs in prehistoric times provided early humans with the flesh of animals and freed our kind from dependency upon the plant life that could only be gathered in limited areas. The ability to hunt game allowed early humans to migrate and to establish new communities beyond the far horizon. However, once those passive fruit collecting, seed-and-root gathering clans of early humans became meat-eaters, there may well have been times when the only flesh available was found in the bodies of other humans. Human wolf packs may have slain members of other clans in order to be among the fittest to survive.

Since we may all be descended from those carnivorous lycanthropes, we must be ever vigilant to keep the beast within firmly shackled with our civilized sense of morality and a deep sense of ourselves as spiritual beings. Some theorists believe that prehistoric members of the human evolutionary family favored the forested areas where they subsisted on leaves and fruits, very much like the great apes. Certain scholars of the human psyche have gone so far as to suggest that there is a portion of our species' latent genetic memory that abhors the shedding of blood and the eating of flesh and feels an unconscious sense of guilt whenever we eat meat. . . .

As you examine the accounts of those who have succumbed to the stirrings of the savage beast within, you may find yourself repelled by lives so twisted by evil. Remember to remain balanced and to emphasize within your own concept of self and soul that you are one with the strengths of community and family and that you cherish the moral values that great spiritual masters have bequeathed to us both by their teachings and by their examples. . . .

A very well-known example of a contemporary werewolf is Jeffrey L. Dahmer, who killed, dismembered, butchered, and ate portions of the flesh of at least 18 human victims. As a modern serial killer, Dahmer portrays the most common and graphic expression of the lycanthrope in today's culture—an individual (almost always male) who leads a double life, then ventures forth sadistically to slash, rip, murder, mutilate, and very often partake of the flesh of his prey. Although much was made of the theory that Dahmer suffered from a mental disease called paraphilia, a sexual attraction to inanimate objects—in his case, dead bodies— the grisly fact remains that he was the sole person responsible for the death of his victims.

Basically a nightstalker, Dahmer would hang around gay bars or shopping malls until closing time, then approach his victim and ask if he would like to accompany him for sex, for drinks, or to take photographs. If the target was somewhat reluctant, Dahmer would not hesitate to offer money as an added inducement. Once he had managed to lure a young man to his apartment, Dahmer would either drug or strangle him, then gradually dismember him.

Thirty-one-year-old Dahmer was arrested on July 24, 1991, when his most recently selected victim, a teenager, managed to escape from the cannibal's apartment and run out into the street, still wearing the handcuffs that were supposed to hold him until Dahmer carved him with a butcher knife. Investigating police officers who first entered the ghastly flat at 213 Oxford Apartments, Milwaukee, Wisconsin, must have felt as if they had descended into one of the lower rings of hell. They discovered nine severed heads—seven in various stages of being boiled; two kept fresh in the refrigerator—four male torsos stuffed into a barrel, and several assorted sections of male genitalia being stored in a pot. Other scraps of human flesh and portions of limbs and bodies were scattered throughout the apartment. The wretched stench of putrefaction was beyond the experience of the most seasoned police officer.

Although generally regarded as a polite, harmless, and quiet young man, Dahmer had a prior police record of a number of minor sex offenses against children. He had been released from prison on probation in 1989 after serving time for having abused a 13-year-old boy. But even dating back to his high school days, Jeffrey Dahmer had been pronounced "a generally weird dude" by his fellow students. In 1989, Dahmer's father had requested that his son receive psychiatric treatment.

Although Jeffrey Dahmer most certainly expressed extremely aberrant behavior, it was argued that he could still distinguish right from wrong. His defense attorney suggested that Dahmer had no awareness that he was mentally ill, he just thought that he occasionally did bad things. The state prosecutor countered by stating that the sadistic cannibal was not possessed of a diseased mind, but a disordered one.

It did seem as though Jeffrey Dahmer was truly suffering from some kind of possession by a terrible beast within his psyche. Throughout the trial, he sat quietly, almost expressionless, as if he had little personal interest in the outcome of the proceedings. On the one hand, he described how he cooked the biceps of one of his victims, seasoned it with salt, pepper, and steak sauce—then, with apparent sincerity, said that he was at a loss to believe that any human being could have done the things that he had done. Before he was sentenced, he rose to make a kind of public apology in which he stated that he had never hoped for his freedom, that he wanted death for himself. Because nearly all of his victims were from minority groups, he wanted it clearly understood that his terrible crimes were not motivated by racial hatreds. Quoting from his statement to the court:

> One of the reasons [that I decided to go through this trial] was to let the world know that these were not hate crimes . . . I wanted to find out just what it was that caused me to be so bad and evil, but most of all . . . I decided that maybe there was a way for us to tell the world that there are people out there with these disorders, maybe they can get help before they end up being hurt or hurting someone. . . . In closing I just want to say that I hope God has forgiven me; I know society will never be able to forgive me for what I have done. . . .

On May 1, 1992, Jeffrey Dahmer was sentenced to life imprisonment on 16 charges of aggravated murder. On November 28, 1994, while he was mopping the bathroom floor in maximum security, Dahmer was killed by Christopher Scarver, a convicted murderer on antipsychotic medication. . . .

William Johnston, alias Harry Meyers, alias Harry Gordon—the sadistic killer of three women—did not claw or bite his victims to death, but he earned the title "The Werewolf of San Francisco" with a straight razor. In the manner of London's Jack the Ripper, Johnston chose prostitutes for his victims.

On the night of April 6, 1935, Betty Coffin turned a corner and started to walk down San Francisco's Market Street. It was 2:30 A.M., and her feet hurt. It was time to call it a night.

Then she saw him. She walked right up to the heavy-set, slightly drunk man, who was dressed like a seaman, and propositioned him. Fifteen minutes later, "Mr. and Mrs. Harry Meyers" had registered in a cheap waterfront hotel.

Two hours later, Meyers came down alone and asked the sleepy night clerk where he could get a beer and a sandwich. The clerk directed him to an all-night greasy spoon diner on the corner.

At eight o'clock the next morning, the maid entered the Meyers's room using her passkey and found the nude, bloody, and battered body of Betty Coffin sprawled on the bed. Her face had been beaten savagely. Her mouth was taped shut. Her body had been ripped open again and again with gaping wounds in regular pattern, as if she had been raked over and over again by the claws of a wild beast, a werewolf. Bloodstained fragments of clothing were strewn about the room.

Inspector Allan McGinn of the San Francisco police told the press that the kind of monster who murders in such a fashion is the type to strike again and again. Newspapers headlined stories of the Werewolf of San Francisco and his brutal and bloody savagery. But the most arduous of police work failed to turn up any clue of the murderer.

Five years passed without another werewolf murder in San Francisco, but Inspector McGinn had been correct about the sadistic human monster working according to some inner cycle of bloodlust. On June 25, 1940, the moon was right for the San Francisco Werewolf to strike again.

The body of Irene Chandler was found in another waterfront hotel in the same condition as that of Betty Coffin. Official causes of death were listed as strangulation and loss of blood, but the corpse bore the same terrible beastlike slashings. The victim was known to the police as a "seagull," a streetwalker who catered to seafaring men. And this time the werewolf had left his "claws" behind—a rusty, bloodstained razor.

The Sailors' Union of the Pacific supplied the police with a picture of the man whom they felt fit the werewolf's general description. On July 8, 1940, a detective confronted Harry W. Gordon at a sailors' union meeting. Gordon was a big, blond man, and the manner in which he had mutilated the two women indicated that he was bestial, cruel, and most likely a psychopath. The detective braced himself for a struggle.

Keeping his voice quiet, hoping to avert violence and to defuse the situation, the detective told Gordon that the police wanted to talk with him at headquarters. Amazingly, the brute who had so hideously carved up two women slumped his shoulders and offered no resistance. Later, after intense questioning, he broke down and confessed to the murders of Betty Coffin and Irene Chandler. The officers were unprepared for Gordon's next confession: "And I killed my first wife in New York, too!"

On September 5, 1941, Harry W. Gordon took his last breath in San Quentin's lethal gas chamber. The savage hunger of the Werewolf of San Francisco was quieted at last. . . .

If law enforcement officers can ever completely substantiate the grisly claims of Henry Lee Lucas, then he would certainly be in the running for the most ruthless and vicious werewolf in history—for his victims would number over 200. The provocative, graphic, and generally unpleasant motion picture *Henry, Portrait of a Serial Killer* (1990) was loosely based on the life and the savage exploits of Lucas.

Finally charged with 11 murders, Lucas has changed his stories many times since he was arrested in May 1983. Demands by the authorities to prove his estimate of a likely 200 victims were often shrugged off by the 47-year-old psychopath with the comment that once he had committed such an act, he simply forgot about it. His first murder, he claims, occurred when he was only 13 and he killed a young female school teacher who rejected his adolescent advances. It is known for certain that he stabbed his mother to death in January 1960 when he was 24.

Lucas was confined to the Ionia State Psychiatric Hospital after being sentenced to 40 years for second-degree murder. Psychiatrists who interviewed him learned that he had been regularly beaten and abused as a child. Henry Lee did, in fact, suffer from frequent dizziness and blackouts because of cruel blows to the head delivered by his mother. Also in his childhood, he had lost his left eye when his brother accidently pierced it with a knife. When doctors ordered X rays of Lucas's skull, they detected extensive damage to the areas of the brain that control behavior and emotion. In assessing the results of their tests of the young outcast, doctors diagnosed Henry Lee Lucas as a psychopath, a sadist, and a sexual deviant.

Then, in spite of such a frightening diagnosis, Lucas was released after he had served only six years of the 40-year sentence. Henry Lee warned them that he should stay locked up. He just knew that it was his nature to kill again.

As if to prove his point in the most dramatic way possible, he murdered a young woman within walking distance of the hospital on the same day that he was let loose upon society.

Lucas figured that he had given the authorities a fair warning. But, rejected once again, he began a savage and brutal campaign of systematic murder and rape that would continue for 17 years and would touch nearly every state in North America. Toward the end of that terrible run, he teamed up for one year with Otis Elwood Toole, a pyromaniac, and Toole's 13-year-old mentally challenged niece Frieda. While Henry Lee raped and killed, Otis would burn, and little Frieda would always be there to service them both during the lulls in their travels.

Lucas was finally apprehended when Otis left to follow his own pyromaniac impulses and he and Frieda decided to settle in the small Texas town of Stoneburg. Lucas got a job as a general handyman to an elderly woman named Kate Rich. Unable to still his perverse instincts to kill, it wasn't long before he had enough of domesticity and regular employment. Suspicious neighbors notified the sheriff that Mrs. Rich and the handyman's "wife" seemed to have disappeared without a trace.

Faced with arrest after his 17-year spree of murder and rape, Lucas showed the police where he had hidden the remains of Mrs. Rich and Frieda. Then, sadly shaking his head, Henry Lee Lucas confessed that he had done some pretty bad things. For at least some of those "pretty bad things," he was sent to Death Row in Huntsville, Texas.

The Werewolf of London

Ed Warren and Lorraine Warren

Currently famous in the area of occult field research, Ed Warren and Lorraine Warren are often called on to investigate paranormal occurrences in places all over the world and are particularly adept at identifying poltergeists, ghosts, and demons. Interestingly, it was their expertise in these areas that drew them to Bill Ramsey, the infamous "Werewolf of London." Ramsey had experienced violent transformations into a wolflike creature since childhood. After repetitive assaults on innocent people, and with medical professionals at a loss to discover any cause for his behavior, Ramsey faced the possibility of life in a mental institution. Yet he was convinced that nothing was wrong with his mind. Married with two children, Ramsey was tortured, hopeless, and afraid he would lose everything. The Warrens were convinced that Ramsey was indeed a werewolf—a cursed man possessed by a demon spirit—and they recommended a traditional exorcism to rid him of the demon. The following excerpt is from their book *Werewolf: A True Story of Demonic Possession* and details several of Ramsey's transformations and attacks from childhood through adulthood. Eyewitnesses testify that not only did Ramsey's behavior change, but during the attacks his appearance changed as well. The Warrens' vivid account of Ramsey's unwilling and recurrent metamorphoses forces the reader to contemplate the possibility that werewolves do indeed exist in the modern world.

Like many imaginative nine-year-olds, Bill Ramsey often liked to play alone. Companions had a way of inhibiting him; with them, he had to play "real" games.

But when he was alone, his mind was free to roam, and he could be anybody from The Man in the Iron Mask to Flash Gordon. . . .

On . . . a sunny Saturday as he recalls, he had come home from the movies and looked forward to two hours of light before night came. He helped his mother with a few chores and then ran outside, eager to play fighter pilot. The matinee that afternoon had run two films about Royal Air Force adventures in World War II, and in his mind Bill was now ensconced in a fighter plane, diving to take out a German bomber destined to set London aflame. . . .

He played for an hour before he turned and felt a coldness come over him like an invisible ocean wave.

To this day, Bill recalls the sensation exactly:

"Have you ever walked into a meat locker right after you've been outside on a hot day? That's what this was like. I was playing and my body temperature was normal and— then . . . well, I'd say it felt as if my body temperature dropped a good twenty degrees. Sweat froze on me. And my whole body started shaking. It was as if I'd opened this door and stepped inside to another dimension or something. And there was this odor. Very foul. A few years earlier, a sewer on our street had backed up. I'd never smelled anything as foul as the gasses that escaped. And that's what this smell was like that afternoon. I was afraid I was going to vomit."

Bill stood in the back yard for a long time trying to make sense of what had happened to him.

He no longer wanted to play.

He felt that he had changed in some subtle, yet profound way. Something terrible had just happened to him, but he had no idea what.

Eventually, the chill left his body and the smell drifted away. He was again a seemingly normal nine-year-old boy standing in the center of his back yard, his curly hair tousled, his body temperature warm again. . . .

He stood staring up at the first of the night's stars, feeling the coldness starting to shudder through him again. He walked slowly over to the fence to look down the narrow alley. If he followed the alley far enough, it would lead him to the sea.

He thought now of stealing aboard a boat—the way young Jim Hawkins had in Robert Louis Stevenson's *Treasure Island*—and sailing somewhere far away where people wouldn't know the truth about him. About the strange coldness inside him now. About the curious, growing rage that seemed to overtake him like a blinding seizure. Images of himself as as wolf began flashing through his mind. . . .

Feelings of Rage

Through the fog of his thoughts and fears, he heard his mother's voice calling him in. Ordinarily, this would have been a comforting thought, a reassurance that the world was a safe, knowable place filled with parents who loved and cared about him and wanted to protect him. But tonight he heard his mother's voice differently. Somehow it irritated him. Didn't she know the truth about him? Didn't she know that he was quite capable of taking care of himself?

He turned, the rage starting to course through him now, and in so doing caught the toe of his shoe against the fence post.

He tripped and fell to the ground.

By the time he'd regained his feet, his anger was blinding him, and he heard the low, chilling rumble of a frenzied beast and knew that, somehow, it was himself he was hearing.

He turned to the fence post, which had been dug and planted deep into the ground, and tore it from its moorings so violently that dirt and grass were flung all the way up on the back porch.

Seeing this, his horrified mother called to his father and they both came running out of the house.

But Bill was too far gone in his rage to stop.

Three men would have had a hard time getting the fence post from the ground. Yet Bill had done it simply and brutally. And now he stood swinging the post over his head as if it were nothing more than a baseball bat. The wire fencing attached to the post was still nailed to the wood.

Worried Parents Try to Help

When his parents drew close and shouted for him to put the post down, Bill hurled it to the ground. But then he fell to his knees and began ripping into the wire fencing with his hands. He pulled the fencing to his teeth and began tearing it apart with them.

His father, terrified by now, tried to pull his son to his feet, but was having a difficult time. The boy's strength was incredible . . . and frightening.

His mother began sobbing.

Finally, hearing the grief he was causing her, Bill relented and forced himself to get back into control.

He threw the fence back to the ground.

His hands and mouth were bloody from where the wire had torn it. In the darkness, all he could hear was his mother's sobbing and his father's confused cursing. And all Bill himself could feel was the peculiar coldness, a coldness at his very center, a coldness that marked him as different from other human beings.

He turned to them then—thinking he was about to say something reassuring—but he was once again seized with the rage.

He saw another image of himself as a wolf.

Another growl started up from his belly and filled his chest and burst out of his mouth.

His mother and father turned and ran back to the house.

The Wolf Emerges

On the back porch, his mother tripped. His father bent to pick her up and when he did so, he looked back at his son and thought he saw—

—a wolf—

And then his parents rushed inside and bolted the door, leaving Bill in the twilit back yard.

Eventually, the roaring quieted, and Bill began to feel the rage leave his body. Some of the coldness left, too, finally. But as he made his way across the back yard up to the porch, he realized that something terrible had happened here to-day, something that could never be undone.

He raised his small hand and started knocking on the back door. His mother and father looked at each other, un-sure if they should let him in. What a strange feeling, to be afraid of your own little boy. . . .

He came running into their arms, the way a much

younger child might. All three of them cried there in the doorway.

Later, as his mother served them dinner, she found herself noticing that Bill had changed in some way—physically. It was a subtle change, one she couldn't really identify. But he had changed in some way of which only a mother would be aware.

They said nothing more of the incident in the yard. Both his parents wanted to believe that it had just been some freakish incident and should be utterly forgotten.

And so it was.

For a few years, anyway. . . .

[Editor's Note: The following events occurred after Bill Ramsey reached adulthood. In this first incident, Ramsey is driving to work late one evening when the symptoms suddenly begin again.]

Bill Ramsey was on his way back to the taxi cab company when he felt a hard pain in the middle of his chest. . . .

Bill pulled his car over to the curb, clutching his chest and trying to get his breathing back to its normal pace. But the pain got worse, and so did the irregularity of his breathing, which now came in great heaves. Cold sweat covered most of his upper body. Terrified that he was going to die, he put the car in gear and headed toward nearby Southend General Hospital.

He went straight to the Emergency Room entrance and found a parking spot. When he got out of the car, another stabbing pain raced up his chest and right arm, and he fell back against the car door. He had a palpable sense that he was dying, that his entire system was shutting down. . . .

By the time he reached the entrance, he was starting to feel the freezing sensation starting up his legs and spreading into his torso. He thought again of his earlier "wolf" episodes. He prayed to God such a thing wasn't happening now. . . .

As soon as Bill opened the door, the nurses glanced up and

saw him. One of the nurses, looking somewhat alarmed, scurried from behind the desk and hurried over to Bill. The other nurse, up on her feet now, too, ran to get a gurney. The nurses carefully helped Bill on to the gurney and then pushed him down a long corridor to a series of empty rooms where emergency patients were treated. . . .

Bill was freezing and asked for a blanket. One of the nurses obliged him. When she finished covering him, she put the blood pressure cuff around his arm and tightened it. . . .

She took his blood pressure. The other nurse wrote down the numbers when they were finished. The first nurse then took his pulse.

"How am I?" Bill said.

Just because he was in a hospital with nurses nearby didn't mean he couldn't still have a heart attack that could kill him on the spot.

"You're fine."

But by the way she said it, Bill could tell that she was simply reassuring him. He had no idea if he were fine or not. . . .

And then he felt the rumbling sensation in his belly.

It started almost like gas pain, moving up through his stomach and into his chest and then into his throat. All the time the sensation moved, it gathered power, so that when it reach his mouth it was expressed in a roar that bounced off the walls and seemed to echo for a good two minutes.

Both nurses jumped back from the gurney. Both looked at Bill in terror. . . .

Awareness of the Change

Bill knew now that he was changing. Images of wolves filled his mind. Wolves slunk low, prowling. Wolves leap on their prey. Wolves mouths dripped hungrily with saliva.

He felt another growl work up from his belly and out his mouth. He felt his hands begin to curl powerfully into paw-like claws. He started to get up from the gurney. . . .

Bill raised himself from the gurney and put one foot on the floor. The first nurse started over to him. She put a hand on his shoulder. . . .

He swiped at her with one of his powerful hands. She jumped back just in time. But this woman was a testament to the entire nursing profession. Instead of deserting Bill, she put her hand on his shoulder again and tried to lay him back down on the gurney. . . .

And Bill allowed himself to be pressed back on the gurney. At least for a few moments. But just as his head was touching the pillow, he let out a horrifying roar again and snapped upward once more.

The Taste of Human Blood

This time, before he knew what he was doing, he grabbed the nurse's arm and dug his teeth into the tender flesh just below the elbow. She screamed. The other nurse, finding her own courage now, came at Bill and slapped at him so he'd let the other nurse go. But at first he didn't let go of her at all. He kept hold of her bleeding arm. The iron-like, tart taste of blood—human blood—filled his mouth. He held on to her arm as if he never planned to let go of it. The other nurse ran out into the hall yelling for help.

At this same time, [a] young policeman had dropped by the hospital for a cup of coffee in the emergency room. The hospital was one of his regular rounds. He always checked to see if there were any way he could help them. . . .

He was just finishing off his coffee when he heard the scream somewhere back in the examining rooms.

The intern he'd been talking to set down his coffee and immediately started running in that direction. The policeman followed closely. Even from here, the policeman could hear furniture being tossed around. The screams of two nurses could also now be heard. And he heard an animal growling.

In his mind, the policeman had a picture of a crazed dog—perhaps a rabid dog had somehow managed to get in here—terrifying some nurses in one of the small examining rooms. He now overtook the intern and led the way into the room.

What he saw, he couldn't believe.

There, crouched in the far corner, was a wild-looking man holding the two nurses at bay. The growls were coming not from some animal, but from the man. . . .

With the way the man crouched, his face slick with sweat and contorted into an animal-like expression, all the policeman could think of was—wolf. . . .

The man, frenzied, glanced wildly around the room. Hatred showed in his eyes when he saw the nurses. He clearly felt they'd betrayed him in some way. The policeman could sense the intern coming up behind him. The intern was a brave lad. Together, they were going to try and capture the wild man. The gurney had restraining straps on it. If they could just get him up there and—

The man picked up another chair and flung it across the room. The nurses screamed again. The policeman and the intern kept inching forward. . . .

A Second Assault

And then the man jumped at him, grabbing the policeman's arm and trying, unmistakably, to bite him.

The low growl was even more chilling this time. The intern used this moment to get behind the man. He got the man's right arm in a hammerlock and shoved him forward to the policeman. Grabbing the man by the shoulder, the policeman shoved him down onto the gurney.

Quickly, the two men lashed him to the cart with restraining straps. They both considered themselves lucky. The man had been so strong they'd barely been able to handle him. And even now, strapped down, it seemed he would eventually be able to snap the straps. He moved so violently inside the straps that the gurney was literally lifted from the floor. . . .

Attacks Cause Problems in Daily Life

There could be no doubt about it. Following the last attack, Bill Ramsey's life changed considerably.

For one thing, there was the scrutiny some of his friends and co-workers applied to him. He felt he was always being evaluated, probed. For another, there was the pressure he put on himself. Any time he felt so much as a head cold coming on, he feared he might be having another attack. . . .

Fortunately, many months went by without another problem occurring. Gradually, the tension Bill sensed in his co-workers vanished, and he could walk around town again without feeling like a criminal. He'd had a problem. Now it was behind him.

He had terrible nightmares, however. The imagery was usually the same. Bill was running down a long, narrow road at dusk. The longer and faster he ran, the less human he looked. Gradually, his upright body became feral, and soon enough he was a timber wolf streaking along the road. . . .

Searching for an Answer

One day Bill was going through Sonia's room at home. His eldest daughter was a nurse at St. Bartholomew's Hospital in London. He found several nursing textbooks she'd left behind. Bill began to search through the textbooks, hoping to find the name of a malady that matched his symptoms.

As Bill tells it, "I used to sneak into her room when nobody was home. I didn't want anybody to know what I was doing. I was afraid it would upset them—you know, we hadn't had a problem in over a year, so why drag them back through everything again? But I was very curious. I began to spend hours with those textbooks, really poring over them.

"I even got to be fairly conversant with medical terms. But no matter how long I read, how hard I looked, I couldn't find anything that described my condition.

"Then one day, I came across the term 'lycanthropy.' At first I didn't know what it meant. I read further and saw that it was described as a "mental condition in which the patient believes he's a werewolf." I could feel my cheeks heat up. I was embarrassed. 'Mental condition' implied that the patient—namely me—was mentally unsound.

"I went to the library and read further. I wanted to see if there were any documented cases in which a person had apparently become a wolf—in fact and not just his imagination.

Shared Experiences

"That was the first time I read about Jean-Paul Grenier, who, in 1798, stole babies from their buggies and literally devoured them. Sometimes he shared his 'feast' with wolves in the surrounding forests. He'd long ago begun to think of himself as a wolf.

"I felt violently ill when I first read about this case. Obviously the youth had been insane—but look where his insanity had led him. Not only did he imagine he was a wolf, he acted on it, by rending the flesh of human infants.

"I felt a real panic. What if my own problem led in this direction? What if, next time—if there was a next time—I not only attacked somebody, but also tried to tear into her with my teeth?

"I tried to convince myself that this was impossible. I had no conscious desire to do what Jean-Paul Grenier had done. Still, in the coming months, that became my nightmare.

"One night I would be walking along a dark street and I

would see a woman coming toward me in the fog—hear the clicking of her high heels on the sidewalk—and I would no longer be able to control myself. I would attack her and rend her flesh.

"I never expressed any of these fears to anybody, though sometimes when I passed by Runwell Mental Hospital I thought of how safe it would be in there—my fears under control, my behavior monitored constantly by the staff.

"But I knew I didn't dare go to Runwell. Only recently had I begun to win back some of the respect I'd lost among my friends. Only recently were people starting to accept me again for the man I used to be. Only recently did I feel that I was a reasonably normal human being again, one who is trustworthy in every respect—despite my nightmares and insecurities.

"And so, even with the knowledge of Jean-Paul Grenier in the back of my mind, I started to relax. I even tried a few nights out with some of my co-workers, stopping for a pint or two of beer after work, and finding that I was completely under control and just another workingman—nothing special.

"And then two years passed. . . .

The Dreams

[One] night I had the nightmare again. Running down a long road at dusk. Turning slowly but surely into a wolf as I ran. Running toward a huge, blood-red moon that lay just behind the gray clouds of dusk.

"I came awake bathed in a sweat so cold, my teeth were literally clacking. I went into the bathroom and found some aspirin. I couldn't stop shaking. I went back to bed and tried to sleep, but I couldn't.

"I lay there until dawn, until it was time to get up for work. I was exhausted. And afraid. I couldn't remember being this frightened in a long time, and I wasn't even sure why. All I knew was that something terrible was going to happen—and soon.". . .

An Eyewitness Account of the Next Attack

On the night of his encounter with Bill Ramsey, Terry Fisher was a twenty-five-year veteran policeman. A big man whose strength is obvious in both his formidable body and in the hard gaze of his eyes, Fisher was known among his fellow officers as a man who could bring virtually any kind of situation under control. . . .

Fisher tells his recollection of that night: "There's really nothing I can say about the incident with Bill Ramsey except that I've never had an experience like it. Several officers and I were inside the precinct when we saw a young woman come through the back door and start to wander around, looking for help. I've seen people in hysteria before—clinical hysteria, I mean—and that's how she looked. Completely frightened, to the point that I was surprised she could even walk.

"We went over to her and asked what was wrong. She couldn't articulate much—just that there was a man outside and that she was terribly afraid of him and that she wanted us to protect her from him. I agreed that I'd go outside and try and find the man and see what was going on. This could be a domestic case, with both parties drinking or taking drugs; or it could be an attempted murder case. She looked so afraid and so upset that I wondered if she was injured in some way. Maybe shock had set in following some trauma.

"I went outside and started looking around. Behind the precinct is a kennel for our dogs. I heard several of them barking. They were upset about something. I went around there and saw this civilian van I'd never seen before. I kept looking around, and then I saw Bill Ramsey. He stood a few feet from the van. He stood very still and just watched me.

"My first impression of him was that he'd been drinking.

He just had that manner. . . . The closer I got, the more I could smell the alcohol on him. I decided I'd ask him to come inside and take a breath test. Most people don't object to that.". . .

A Sense of Something Wrong

"He just watched me. Now that I'd been out here a while, I began to sense how strange he looked. There was something not quite human in the eyes, particularly. For the first time, I started to feel a little nervous. . . .

"I put out my hand to take his elbow and guide him into the station. He jerked away from me, very angry. By now, he was muttering things to himself, but I couldn't understand. Behind him now, the dogs were barking furiously, very upset. I'd never seem them react to a person as they did to Bill. . . .

When I touched his elbow again, he once more jerked away. A kind of low rumbling started up in his chest and rose to his throat. At first, I thought I'd confused this with one of the dogs growling. Then I realized it was Bill Ramsey. He attacked me then. There's no other way to say it, and it was just that simple. I was standing there and he attacked me."

An Attack on the Policeman

"Before I knew what was happening, he threw me to the ground and got on top of me. His face underwent an incredible transformation. His eyes got especially crazy. His lip pulled back over his teeth and his hands suddenly became claw-like. He was tearing at me the way an animal would, as if he was trying to rend my flesh.

"I'm a big man, and a strong one. Many times during my quarter-century with the police department, I've been called to help stop violent situations. I can get very physical when I need to, and I've certainly been up against my share of mean drunks.

"But Bill Ramsey was different. I couldn't seem to slow him down. We wrestled there on the ground, and he kept clawing at me and ripping at me. I tried to get him into various kinds of restraining positions, but I couldn't budge him. The amazing thing was that he kept getting stronger the longer we wrestled on the ground.

"His anger was starting to take its toll. I could feel him starting to do real damage to me, especially to my back, as he pounded me again and again against the ground. And then he got his hands on my throat and started strangling me. There's no other way to say it: I could literally feel the life begin to drain out of me. I looked up and saw the absolute glee in his eyes. He knew he was killing me, and he was delighted about it.

"I tried to push my hands up to his own throat, to stop him, but it didn't work. Not only was the life draining from me, but fear was starting to paralyze me. That had never happened to me in all my time as a police officer. I'd heard about it, of course, how fear at just the right moment can immobilize a person, but it had been beyond my comprehension. I'd always smugly thought that this could never happen to me. If I ever got in a situation like this, my survival instinct would take over. But it didn't—Bill Ramsey continued to strangle me.

"I started losing consciousness.

'When the Devil's in me, I'm strong!' he kept saying over and over again. It was like a religious chant. And the longer he said it, the stranger his face got, especially his eyes, and the stronger he became.

"Blackness started swimming before my eyes. I felt a deep chill run through my body. His voice got fainter and fainter. I realized that I was dying, and that I could do absolutely nothing about it. Right there in the police station parking lot, Bill Ramsey was going to kill me. I started blacking out . . ."

Chapter 2

Fact or Fiction?

Tracking the Werewolf: Arguments Against the Existence of Werewolves

Eyewitness Accounts of Werewolves Can Be Explained

Daniel Farson

Daniel Farson has an interesting tie to the world of the supernatural: He is the great-nephew of Bram Stoker, the author of *Dracula*. In his book *The Supernatural: Vampires, Zombies, and Monster Men*, from which the following essay is taken, Farson uncovers the reasons he believes certain superstitions have held such power over the human race throughout history. In this excerpt Farson explores common superstitions about werewolves. These range from the seemingly impossible belief that werewolves hid their hair on the inside of their bodies to the belief that werewolves were in fact witches and warlocks, chosen minions of the devil. Farson argues that these beliefs are simple superstitions designed to explain away a very real, but perhaps irrational, human fear of wolves. In primitive times wolves were more numerous than they are today—in fact, wolves are extinct in many places in the world due to hunting and the expansion

Daniel Farson, *The Supernatural: Vampires, Zombies, and Monster Men*. London: Aldus Books Limited, 1975. Copyright © 1975 by Aldus Books Limited. Reproduced by permission.

of civilization. Farson also points out that the belief in werewolves is tied to man's own primitive past, suggesting that the belief arose out of a desire to explain the often brutal and animalistic behavior of which humans are capable. Farson's explanations provide strong evidence that the figure of the werewolf is just another creation of the human mind, a symbol of that which we most fear to see in ourselves.

In the year 1598, in a remote patch of forest in Western France, an archer and a group of armed countrymen came across the naked body of a boy. The corpse had been horribly mutilated and torn. The limbs, still warm and palpitating, were drenched with blood. As the Frenchmen approached the body, they caught sight of what appeared to be two wolves running off between the trees. The men gave chase, but to their amazement, they found they had caught, not a wolf, but what proved to be a man—tall, gaunt, clothed in rags, and with matted, verminous hair and beard. To their horror they noticed that his hands were still stained with fresh blood, and his claw-like nails clotted with human flesh. The man, it turned out, was a wandering beggar named Jacques Roulet, and he was brought to trial at the town of Angers in August 1598. And if the discovery of Roulet was a shock to the people of Angers, the trial proceedings were shattering.

Roulet confessed to the court: "I was a wolf."

"Do your hands and feet become paws?"

"Yes, they do."

"Does your head become like that of a wolf?"

"I do not know how my head was at the time; I used my teeth."

In reaching their verdict the court had to decide whether

Roulet was a werewolf, as he claimed, or a lycanthrope, which is related but different. A werewolf or werwolf is a living person who has the power to change into a wolf. The word comes from Old English *wer*, meaning man, and wolf. A *lycanthrope* is someone suffering from a mental illness that makes him believe he is transformed into a wolf. This word comes from the Greek for wolfman. In either case, Roulet could have faced execution. But the court showed a compassion rare for its time. Judging Roulet to be mentally sick—and therefore a lycanthrope—they sentenced him to a madhouse for only two years.

Common Beliefs and Superstitions

A true werewolf was generally believed to undergo an almost complete transformation into a wolf, unlike the werewolf of Hollywood movies who remains basically human in appearance. Much controversy arose in the past over people who were said to disguise the fact that they were wolves by wearing their fur on the inside. It was claimed that such people looked ordinary enough, but that their skin was inside out. When they were torn apart—as hundreds of innocent people were at various times in past centuries—the hair, or wolf fur, could be seen on the other side of the skin. . . .

Anyone who ate the flesh of a sheep killed by a wolf was liable to become a werewolf. A person who ate a wolf's brains or drank water from his footprints was certain to become one. In some places, eating certain large and sweet smelling flowers or drinking from a stream where a wolfpack had drunk was a sure way to turn into a wolf.

Anybody with small pointed ears, prominent teeth, strong curved fingernails, bushy eyebrows that met over the nose, a third finger as long as the second on each hand, or even a lot of hair—especially on the hands and feet—was immediately suspect. However, if you are tempted to take a closer look at your friends next time you see them, remember that the eyes of a werewolf always remain human. . . .

These beliefs stemmed from people's ignorant fear of anyone who was different. In some traditions it was easy to become a werewolf by accident. In others, you had to be especially evil to merit such a fate. Some tales suggest that a bestial person would return after death as a wolf. Ghostly werewolves, however, are extremely rare in folklore. . . . The werewolf is very much a living person, and more akin to the witch in that he or she may actively seek to become a werewolf. This can be done by entering into a pact with a demon known as the Wolf Spirit or with the Devil himself. . . .

The man or woman who has achieved the power of metamorphosis will change into a wolf at sunset every night until death, reassuming human shape at dawn. Some folk tales say that the werewolf must roll in the dirt or the morning dew in order to change back into a human; others that the transformation occurs automatically at daybreak. A werewolf that is wounded or killed immediately becomes human again. Usually the creature can be caught or destroyed like an ordinary wolf, but the most effective way of killing a werewolf is to shoot it with a silver bullet. The corpse must then be burned rather than buried.

Reasons for the Belief in Werewolves

To most people all this sounds like a welter of primitive superstition, and it is significant that reports of werewolves decreased as cities spread into the countryside. Such tales have always been commonest in remote regions where the wolf was the foremost beast of prey. Today, when the wolf has all but disappeared from the United States and many European countries, it may be hard for us to imagine the terror this animal inspired in our ancestors. In northern countries especially, the wolf was a deadly enemy, hated and feared for its ferocious attacks on flocks and people alike. But the wolf also seemed eerie, moving mainly by night, ghostly gray and silent, almost invisible except for the slanting eyes that glowed red by firelight and yellow-green by moonlight. Add to this its spine-chilling howl—said to be an omen of death—and it is not surprising that the wolf came to be regarded as an evil, almost supernatural monster. Wherever there were wolves there were also reports of werewolves, whom people feared with a panic verging on hysteria. . . .

A Long History of Belief

Reports of werewolves have been documented all over the world since ancient times. As early as the 5th century B.C. Herodotus, who is known as the "father of history," wrote: "Each Neurian changes himself once a year into the form of a wolf and he continues in that form for several days, after which he resumes his former shape." In the 2nd century A.D. a Roman doctor observed that "lycanthropia is a species of melancholy which can be cured at the time of the attack by opening a vein and abstracting blood."

Petronius, the 1st-century Roman satirist, tells a werewolf story with a universal theme. It concerns a servant who accompanied a soldier on a night's journey out of town, and was aghast to see him strip off his clothes by the roadside and change into a wolf. With a howl the creature leaped into the woods and disappeared from view. When the servant reached his destination, he was told that a wolf had just broken into the farm, and had savaged the cattle before being driven away by a man who had thrust a pike into the animal's neck. Hurrying home at daybreak, the servant came to the place where the soldier's clothes had been, but he found only a pool of blood. Back home, the soldier lay wounded with a doctor dressing his neck.

This epitomizes a constant theme of the werewolf legend:

the wolf is wounded in a fight and a human being is later discovered suffering from the same wound. A story from the Middle Ages tells of a Russian noblewoman who doubted that anyone could change into an animal. One of her servants volunteered to prove her wrong. He changed into a wolf and raced across the fields, chased by his mistress's dogs, which cornered him and damaged one of his eyes. When the servant returned to his mistress in human form he was blind in one eye. . . .

Ties to Man's Primitive Roots

The concept of a man or woman turning into a wolf is no more outrageous than that of a corpse emerging from the coffin at night to drink human blood. Yet it is somehow even harder to believe in werewolves than in vampires. This may be partly because the werewolf fits so neatly into folklore. The monstrous wolfman made the ideal character for a good horror tale to tell around the fire in remote regions, where there was little to talk about apart from the wild animals of the forest and perhaps the even wilder characters in the village. Werewolves were alleged to be especially partial to small boys and girls, so they would serve as a natural threat for the peasants to their children. "Don't go out in the woods tonight or the werewolf will gobble you up," they might say, just as London Cockneys warned their children not to roam the streets of the East End after the murders of 1888 "or Jack the Ripper will get you."

But the belief in werewolves has deeper roots. The metamorphosis of men into animals is part of primeval legend, a power attributed to the gods and heroes of mythology. The Scandinavian god Odin turned into an eagle; Jupiter, the Roman god, became a bull; Actaeon was changed into a stag by the Greek goddess Artemis. There are counterparts of the werewolf in almost all parts of the world, varying according to climate: were-tigers in India; were-leopards, were-hyenas, and even were-crocodiles in Africa; and were-bears in Russia, which also had its fair share of werewolves. . . . Significantly, were-animals are always creatures that inspire fear; you never hear of a were-tortoise.

The *berserkers*—ancient Norse warriors who fought with murderous frenzy—exploited the fearsome reputation of wild animals by wearing bearskins in battle. These gangs of Nordic fighters would work themselves into a state of diabolical madness as they hurled themselves into the attack, howling like animals and foaming at the mouth. Our word *berserk*, meaning violently enraged, comes from the *bear sark*—bearskin—the berserkers wore. Just as the word lives on, so the memory of these barbaric warriors may have contributed to the werewolf legend. To the peaceful villagers whose community was attacked one day by fur-clad berserkers and another by a pack of howling wolves, there can have seemed little enough difference between the two. Both might have seemed like men dressed as animals—or like men completely transformed into raging beasts.

The Origins of the Myth and the Human Psyche

Others trace the werewolf legend back further still to the time when prehistoric man began to don animal disguise for the hunt, and to invoke the spirit of a powerful animal in the hope of inheriting that animal's strength. In his book *Man Into Wolf* Dr. Robert Eisler, a British writer with a profound knowledge of ancient history and legend, develops a fascinating theory of the origins of the werewolf idea. Eisler's explanation starts with the idea that man was once a peaceful vegetarian, but was driven to seek new food by changing conditions—such as the arrival of an Ice Age. He was forced to eat meat, to cover himself with animal skins, to hunt, and to imitate the behavior of ferocious wild animals in his struggle to survive. Gradually man himself acquired the same blood lust, probably even turning to cannibalism in times of extreme food shortage. This traumatic upheaval left its scars that lingered on in man's unconscious, says Eisler, giving rise among other things to the werewolf legend.

There are also more straightforward explanations. Furs were worn in winter as a protection against cold, and a fur-clad figure might easily be mistaken for an animal. Werewolves might have been children who had been lost or abandoned in the forest, raised by a pack of wolves, and therefore practicing all the skills of the wild animal. But Eisler's theory is still the most attractive. Writing about the concept of *metempsychosis*—the passing of a soul from one body to another after death—[Sabine] Baring Gould refers to "the yearnings and gropings of the soul after the source whence its own consciousness was derived, counting its dreams and hallucinations as gleams of memory, recording acts which had taken place in a former state of existence."

To some extent this echo exists in us all. The counterpart of the female vamp is the male wolf—a man who pushes his attentions on women—and he is still with us today, complete with wolf whistle. The werewolf is a monster of the unconscious, "the beast within" that may still emerge in our dream life. American psychoanalyst Dr. Nandor Fodor has recorded a number of dreams reported by patients in which the werewolf theme figures prominently, complete with all the brutal details of transformation, savage attack, and killing.

At its fiercest extreme, however, this primeval instinct is seen most clearly in the secret societies of the Leopard Men in West Africa, who continue to disguise themselves as leopards up to the present day. Although it is most unlikely that man can change into wolf, it is certain that man frequently imitates the wildest of animals, even to assuming their skins.

Rabies Epidemics Explain Werewolf Sightings

Ian Woodward

Noted British researcher Ian Woodward is well known by occult and paranormal historians for his book *The Werewolf Delusion*, from which the following essay is taken. In the book Woodward explores the various ambiguities and inconsistencies in the werewolf myth in an effort to discover the truth about this mysterious creature. In this essay, he makes a strong case for werewolves as victims of mistaken identity. Basing his argument on thorough research and comparative analysis, Woodward asserts that rabies epidemics might be at the heart of the werewolf myth. He systematically presents medical evidence comparing symptoms of human rabies with those experienced by individuals believed to be werewolves. After discussing the various ways rabies can be transmitted to humans, Woodward points out that human rabies can occur in epidemic proportions in a cyclical manner, meaning they tend to reoccur in history over time. He arrives at the conclusion that it is indeed a possibility that epidemics of rabies, either in wolves or in humans, could coincide with epidemics of werewolf sightings in history, thereby providing a reasonable explanation for eyewitness accounts of werewolves.

In the autumn of 1976, at the North Manchester General Hospital in England, a fifty-three-year-old chef spent his last hours enduring periods of diabolical horror. "He looked like a scared animal," said a doctor. The man, Mohammed Muslim, who died of rabies, was bitten earlier in the year by a dog while visiting his family in Bangladesh. In hospital he displayed the following symptoms: he foamed at the mouth, he screamed uncontrollably, and he bit a nurse; at one point it took five strong men to get him up off the floor, so immense was his rabid strength. The supervising physician explained how the patient's "uncontrollable screaming attacks" were unabated by the use of drugs which would have sedated an ordinary patient.

The symptoms experienced by Mohammed Muslim during his "attacks," symptoms shared by hundreds of other victims of rabies, today and in former times, point irrefutably to one unavoidable conclusion: that a certain proportion of the many early eye-witness accounts of werewolves did, in fact, pertain to human sufferers in various stages of *rabies canina*. Dryness of the tongue, inordinate thirst, an abhorrence of water, foaming at the mouth, superhuman strength, violent tendencies—these are some of the symptoms common to both the werewolf and the victim of *rabies canina* in human beings, the latter being bitten by rabid dogs or wolves, and driven themselves to bite others.

Rabies Symptoms Are Characteristic of Werewolves

Frothing at the mouth, which characterizes the human rabid patient, has been a distinguishing factor of the werewolf for thousand of years. . . . The foaming jaws, the animal rages, the crooked limbs, the savage eyes, the rabid countenance—these are the symptoms of one of the most terrifying and hideous diseases ever to afflict humanity. . . . A rabid wolf, the head and jaws all splattered with foam, is a frightening enough sight; but the wild ferocity of its attack on man is chilling in the extreme. Being bitten by a werewolf, according to some traditions, will make the victim a werewolf. Being bitten by a rabid wolf will also surely make the victim rabid. To the rustic mind, a rabid wolf would more than likely be seen as a werewolf, especially if that person was attacked by the diseased animal and subsequently developed all the symptoms of rabies.

Rabies Is Transmitted in Various Ways

Rabies, which is the Latin word for madness, is usually spread to a victim in a violent tooth-and-claw manner, the virus itself being transmitted by acutely infectious saliva; having been deposited in the tissues of the victim, the virus can then start its cycle of infection and multiplication. But it can also be transmitted by the infected saliva coming into contact with cut or split skin or even undamaged mucous membrane, including the eyelids, mouth, nose, anus, and external genital organs, as well as through eating infected food or drinking infected water. To drink water out of the footprint made by a werewolf, or to drink from a lycanthropous pool, was said to transmit the disease of werewolfery to the drinker. So could not the "lycanthropous pool" be little more than a water-hole frequented by rabid animals? And as wolves fastidiously lick their paws after eating a meal, could not the footprints be simply the saliva-infected impressions of rabid wolves? If such was the case, it would certainly help to explain the origin of one aspect of the werewolf legend.

Historical accounts also talk of lycanthropes who go about their morbid business only at night; or, if during the day, only in places which are heavily shaded, such as dense forests. Since in some cases of rabies the human patient experiences an extreme sensitivity to bright light, it could well be that at least a few of the past's reported lycanthropes were in fact people suffering, in varying degrees, from this disease. The rabies victim would certainly choose darkness as the most convenient period in the day for venturing out of doors.

Feats of Strength and Fear of Water

There is then the question of the extraordinary strength and periods of violent spasms shared by the human and animal rabies victim. . . . A human rabid patient (including a child) frequently has moments when an increase in strength is so marked that it requires five people to hold him down. Historical accounts of the werewolf often refer to its extraordinary strength, and to the fact that several people who have gone to a victim's rescue have been powerless to overcome the beast's brute savagery and physical toughness. In the Middle Ages a rabid wolf such as this, if it got away, would certainly pass into werewolfic legend—as would the victims if they contracted the disease and developed the symptoms of the werewolf/rabid patient. According to Geoffrey P. West in his *Rabies: In Animals and Man* (1972) these symptoms include:

> a feeling of apprehension; a burning or tingling sensation at the site of the bite; an excess of saliva in the mouth (so that the patient may be constantly spitting); intermittent mental derangement, which may be associated with periods of mania, when bedclothes may be torn to shreds; pain; and con-

vulsions. The name "hydrophobia" (meaning fear of water, but used in past centuries as a synonym for the illness) derives from the horror which the mere sight of water can bring to the human patient, who may suffer agonising muscular spasms if he attempts to drink.

Rabies Causes Wolflike Barking

A subsidiary symptom of a hydrophobic patient's repulsion of water—or indeed *any* liquid—is an hysterical barking sound: very similar, by all accounts, to the terrible "barking" which many werewolves in their human shape were said to make. David A. Warrell, consultant physician and clinical lecturer in tropical medicine at the Radcliffe Infirmary, Oxford, describes in *Rabies: The Facts* (1977) the progression of symptoms which eventually climax with the characteristic barking:

> Patients show an extraordinary ambivalence about drinking. They avoid drinking for some time, fearing the effects, but finally become unbearably thirsty. Attempts to lift the cup to their lips are thwarted by violent trembling of the arm. They try desperately to snatch a sip of water before a last-minute terror makes them fling away the cup and dive under the bedclothes. During spasms the drink or saliva may be spat or coughed out in showers over bystanders. Patients may retch or vomit so violently that tears are made in the gullet near its junction with the stomach. Cries of alarm may be distorted by paralysis or swelling of the vocal cords which alter the voice so that the shouts sound more like barks.

> At the peak of an attack the whole nervous system seems to be aroused. The patient is in a state of extreme agitation and has frightening hallucinations. His face is a mask of terror. His body is racked with tremors or spasms. He may struggle frantically to free himself and try to escape from the room.

. . . Many werewolves in the past were said to lock themselves in a room when they felt their ravening spasms approaching. I wonder, though, whether or not this has been twisted in the telling? It may well be that it was those nearest to the "werewolf," fearing for their own safety as a consequence of his impending mad rages, who locked him in the room. If the "werewolf" was in fact a victim of rabies or hydrophobia, they had every reason to fear him and to take all necessary precautions.

Rabies Epidemics: Past and Present

Historical documentation shows that the incidence of rabies rises and falls in cycles of roughly one hundred years, a century of epidemic being separated by a century of relative calm. We are now living at a time when the disease is rapidly building up to explosive proportions. A conservative estimate of worldwide deaths from rabies today is thirty thousand, of which India alone accounts for half this figure. Rabies was certainly raging in the Middle Ages, especially between 1500 and 1600—and so, of course, was werewolfery; and although foxes, badgers, bears and other animals were also affected, people most feared rabid wolves (not that the country people necessarily *knew* they were rabid) because of the sheer savagery and unpredictable nature of their character. A great many of the reported werewolves were undoubtedly rabid wolves: sufficient in number (as indeed were their rabid human victims) to sow the seed for many a good werewolf story. . . .

One further point of interest is that France has a history of periodic rabies going back at least a thousand years. A new cycle of the disease began in the north-eastern region of the country in 1968 and has been spreading west and south ever since. Significantly, the area so far covered by the spread of rabies in France is identical to those areas most afflicted with werewolfery in the sixteenth and seventeenth centuries. In the nearby Jura region, well-known for its werewolfic associations, an epidemic of animal rabies raged there between 1803 and 1835, subsequently spreading throughout Switzerland; it had already reached Germany by

1820. Rabid wolves were attacking the inhabitants of Crema, Italy, in 1804, from which many died; other rabid wolves in France in 1851, in Turkey in 1852, Russia in 1866, and elsewhere, attacked and subsequently caused the deaths of many people through rabies . . . in earlier times, I am certain, an accusatory finger would have been pointed at many a werewolf. It is also possible, of course, that genuine werewolves might be misdiagnosed as rabies victims, the symptoms being caused by the transformation rituals and the werewolf's psychological make-up. The restriction of salivation and the drying-up of the tear-ducts, in the case of werewolves who have participated in black-magic transformation ceremonies, can be accounted for by the drugs they used. Henbane and stramonium, for instance, with which initiate werewolves drugged themselves in order to evoke soaring and flying dreams, produced a sensational dual-condition: first an abhorrence of water while the werewolf is in his animal form, and then an insatiable thirst when he returns to his normal human shape. . . .

I have no doubt that, because of the shared symptoms, a vast proportion of history's dreaded "werewolves" were in fact either rabid wolves or their rabid human victims. The facts seem to speak for themselves.

The Werewolf Disease

Basil Copper

A well-known and highly respected writer of mystery and horror novels, Basil Copper was born in London in 1924. His love of all things mysterious led him to write *The Vampire in Legend, Fact, and Art* in 1974 to explore the reasons behind the fascination with these dark and evil creatures. This was closely followed by *The Werewolf in Legend, Fact, and Art* in 1977. In *The Werewolf*, Copper traces the history of the werewolf legend by bringing together a wide variety of sources to separate the truth from the fiction.

In the following excerpt from *The Werewolf*, Copper presents the amazing research done by Dr. Lee Illis, who argues that people who were suspected of being werewolves actually suffered from an extremely rare medical condition called congenital porphyria. Illis's work is based on careful analysis of eyewitness accounts, court documents, and personal testimonies of werewolf victims as well as those accused of being werewolves, their legal representatives, and evaluating medical officials. To ensure his research was thorough, Illis gathered evidence from different time periods and from various places throughout the world. Based on his analysis, the doctor concludes that it is possible to explain at least some portion of the werewolf phenomenon through the parallels he establishes between the symptoms of porphyria sufferers and the behaviors and appearance of those suspected of being werewolves. The argument may be made that this explanation is too simple and that since the disease is so rare, it cannot possibly explain instances of werewolves existing the world over. However, the evidence presented by the doctor is compelling, and the similarities between the two conditions tend to make a strong case that is worthy of critical consideration.

The novelist Sir Walter Scott recognized the difficulties and touched on the terrors of lycanthropy in one of his less familiar works, *Demonology and Witchcraft*, which was published by John Murray in 1830 as part of an eighty-volume collection called *Murray's Family Library*. . . .

In it, he wrote shrewdly of the werewolf but for the most part contented himself with repeating other people's opinions. Of this curse which laid waste Europe he said, "Lycanthropy, a superstition which was chiefly current in France, but was known in other countries and is the subject of great debate. . . .

"The idea . . . was that a human being had the power, by sorcery, of transforming himself into the shape of a wolf, and in that capacity, being seized with a species of fury, he rushed out and made havoc among the flocks, slaying and wasting, like the animal whom he represented, far more than he could devour.

"The more incredulous reasoners would not allow of a real transformation, whether with or without the enchanted hide of a wolf, which in some cases was supposed to aid the metamorphosis, and contended that lycanthropy only subsisted as a woeful species of disease, a melancholy state of mind, broken with occasional fits of insanity, in which the patient imagined that he committed the ravages of which he was accused."

Scott was in error though, when he supposed that lycanthropy was heard of no more after the time of Louis XIV. But he showed remarkable prescience in some of his observations. Though he was referring to ghost stories, his remarks apply equally to the werewolf when he observes (of the public), "They want evidence. It is true that the general wish to believe, rather than the power of believing, has given certain stories some such currency in society.". . .

An English doctor in modern times has put forward a remarkably convincing explanation for the 'werewolf disease' which afflicted Europe in the Middle Ages and in other periods. We shall now proceed to examine his thesis. . . .

Werewolves Suffer from Porphyria

Dr [Lee] Illis' paper, "On Porphyria and the Aetiology of Werwolves" [October 1963], is a well-documented and, to my mind, unassailable argument to the effect that the outbreaks of lycanthropy which afflicted Europe and other parts of the world at various times had a solid medical basis.

Dr Illis, who prefers the term 'werwolf', says, "I believe that the so-called werwolves of the past may, at least in the majority of instances, have been suffering from congenital porphyria. The evidence for this lies in the remarkable relation between the symptoms of this rare disease and the many accounts of werwolves that have come down to us."

After dealing with instances of classical history and legend, . . . he adds, "The transformation into a wolf is not exclusive to men. Armenian and Abyssinian legends clearly implicate women and [Henri] Boguet, a sixteenth-century judge who was responsible for the burning of about six hundred witches and werwolves, recounts the story of a farmer's wife who changed into a wolf and attacked a neighbour.". . .

Werewolf Symptoms Similar to Porphyria

Later the doctor observes in developing his thesis, "A Borussian werwolf was brought before the Duke of Prussia, and John Frederic Wolfeshusius of Leipzig University (1591) describes him: "He was an evil-favoured man, not much unlike a beast, and he had many scars on his face . . . although he was long and vigilantly watched, this werwolf never cast what little he possessed of human shape."

And Dr Illis adds, "Amongst the Toradja natives of Celebes (Dutch East Indies), werwolves are described as having unsteady eyes with dark green shadows under them. They do not sleep soundly. They have a long tongue with red lips and teeth which remain red in spite of chewing betel nuts. Their hair stands on end.

"Boguet describes werwolves as having a pale skin with numerous excoriations from frequenting with wolves or perhaps as a consequence of their attacks on human beings. One, he writes, was so disfigured as to be scarcely recognizable as a human being, and people could not regard him without shuddering."

The physical descriptions of these people are extremely important to the Illis theory and it should be noted that they correspond exactly to the physical symptoms of the extreme forms of porphyria as known to medical science. . . .

"It is difficult to build up a picture of a werwolf, but the most consistent one would be of a man, or occasionally a woman or child, who wanders about at night. The skin is pale, with a yellowish or greenish tint, with numerous ex-coriations, and with a red mouth. The eyes are unsteady.". . .

Reasons Why People Believe in Werewolves

"A belief so widespread both in time and place as that of the werwolf must have some basis in fact. Either werwolves exist or some phenomenon must exist or have existed on which, by the play of fear, superstition and chance, a legend was built and grew.

"Tracing the origins of the werwolf myth is a difficult exercise. One is continually met with conflicting evidence. There would seem to be two suggestions for the origin of this myth. One is that it is a result of fear, and an invocation of evil spirits, or near witchcraft, to account for some strange happenings which could not be explained by the contemporary philosophies.

"This is attractive but, by itself, carries us no further. It cannot explain the widespread belief and it makes no contribution to the exact aetiology of the fear. My suggestion is that the myth arose in several isolated areas in various parts of the world, as a result of some rare, but widespread happenings, and spread into the common consciousness.". . .

"Although essentially a pre-Christian belief based on the need to externalize fear, once a story of a werwolf of sufficient credibility was established, it would persist for several generations and become the focus of explaining other dreadful and otherwise inexplicable happenings. Indirect help would come from the religious teachings of the time which played strongly upon the ignorance and credulity of the uneducated."

Porphyria Offers a Reasonable Explanation

Congenital porphyria is a rare disease, as already stated, but it may be that when a person in the Middle Ages became affected by it, his subsequent actions were seen by the authorities as bearing the taint of lycanthropy. It needed only one case for a whole district to become infected with a collective hysteria, in which neighbour denounced neighbour.

What then are the symptoms and the outward manifestations of this rather strange disease? Dr Illis explains that porphyria is caused by a recessive gene which leads to "severe photosensitivity in which a vesicular erythema is produced by the action of light."

Or in layman's terms a sensitivity of the skin which is so affected by light, particularly sunlight, that the patient breaks out in a superficial, patchy inflammation.

Illis observes, "The urine is often reddish-brown as a result of the presence of large quantities of porphyrins. There is a tendency for the skin lesions to ulcerate and these ulcers may attack cartilage and bone. Over a period of years structures such as nose, ears, eyelids and fingers undergo progressive mutilation."

Other effects of porphyria are pigmentation of the skin; and the teeth may be red or reddish-brown due to the deposit of porphyrins. As the reader may have noted, some of these medical symptoms are the classical signs by which the lycanthrope has been identified throughout the ages.

The wandering about at night, which the victim of porphyria would find more bearable than exposure to daylight; the excoriations and lesions to the skin of the face and hands, typical of the werewolf who had been bitten by wild animals; and possible nervous manifestations; all would have been enough, in medieval times, to condemn such a poor wretch to the execution block as a proven werewolf.

Significantly, Dr Illis postulates, "The nervous manifestations may be referable to any part of the nervous system, and include mental disorders, ranging from mild hysteria to manic-depressive psychoses and delirium. Epilepsy may occur.". . .

Dr Illis concludes, "It is possible, then, to paint a picture of a porphyric which, though not necessarily characteristic or typical, will fit with all the available evidence in the literature of porphyria; such a person, because of photosensitivity and the resultant disfigurement, may choose only to wander about at night. . . .

"In ancient times this would be accentuated by the physical and social treatment he received from the other villagers, whose instincts would be to explain the apparition in terms of witchcraft or Satanic possession."

Parallel Between Porphyria Sufferers and Werewolf Victims

The clinical behaviour of sufferers from porphyria as outlined by Dr Illis in his original paper, exactly parallels those of the werewolf victims of which we have earlier spoken: the rough and broken skin; the yellowish and distorted features; even the hair, which might well have been the result of natural reluctance to shave when suffering from such painful skin disorders; and the night wanderings. All these are the classic hallmarks of the werewolf of legend and of the medieval trials.

Add to this mental disorder and other disturbances, and the resultant confusion of such a poor wretch when hunted through the night; captured and possibly manhandled; and then finally brought before a magistrate or ecclesiastical commission. Small wonder that such "lycanthropes" were more than eager to confess to something they did not understand, even if only to alleviate their current sufferings.

What is the cause of this extreme form of porphyria and is it confined only to a comparatively few parts of the world, it might be asked. It is important to emphasize from the outset that the type of porphyria discussed by Dr Illis in his paper and which we are currently dealing with . . . is an extremely rare condition and should not be confused with a common and widespread type which has nothing whatever to do with the subject of lycanthropy.

Dr Illis explains, "There are several types of porphyria and nearly all these types have a genetic basis. They are due to a metabolic disorder; or another way of describing them is that they are due to an inborn error of metabolism. One type of porphyria is relatively common and occurs in all countries, including Great Britain. This is *not* the type which has anything to do with the werewolf myth.

"I think this should be emphasized otherwise it would cause unnecessary suffering to people who have this type of porphyria. The type of porphyria which may possibly account for the origin of the werwolf myth is a *very rare* type of the disorder often known as congenital porphyria."

The Werewolf: A Symbol of Humanity's Animal Past

Ernest Jones

A psychoanalyst who worked closely with Sigmund Freud, Ernest Jones is most well known for his book *On the Nightmare*, from which the following excerpt is taken. In the book Jones argues that the monsters and fantasies that populate our superstitions, myths, and folklore originate in the unconscious mind. Humans create these monsters as a way to help explain, or place responsibility for, repressed desires and fears created by extreme emotions of love or hate, with hate being the emotion most closely symbolized by the werewolf. Acting on these desires or fears would mean admitting that a dark, or less socially acceptable, side of human nature exists. For human beings, the werewolf might be the most feared and perhaps the most highly symbolic of these nightmare monsters as it represents not only man's ties to his primitive past but also the animalistic tendencies he still possesses in spite of his civilized existence. Jones argues that this imbalance causes a great deal of anxiety in the human psyche. Anxiety about human tendencies toward sadistic, brutal, and cruel acts gives rise to the image of the werewolf in dreams and mythologies. According to Jones, the werewolf as a monstrous animal is a fiction; that the human mind is adept at creating and believing in vivid dream images to escape responsibility for its own monstrous and animalistic tendencies is a fact.

The conception of the Werewolf is one of the most developed examples of the belief in the transformation of men into animals. . . . The other most important elements in this superstition are flight by night and cannibalism.

The wolf belongs to the group of savage animals which have been extensively employed in mythology and folklore for the portrayal of cruel and sadistic phantasies. To the same class as Werewolves belong the men-hyenas of Abyssinia, the men-leopards of South Africa, the men-tigers of Hindustan, the men-bears of Scandinavia, in whose existence . . . the Norwegian peasants still believe. . . .

The most prominent attributes which we may expect to have been used for the purposes of symbolism are thus swiftness of movement, insatiable lust for blood, cruelty, a way of attacking characterized by a combination of boldness and cunning craftiness, and further the associations with the ideas of night, death and corpse. As is easy to see, the savage and uncanny features characteristic of the wolf have made him specially suited to represent the dangerous and immoral side of nature in general and of human nature in particular. These features explain why the wolf has played a considerable part in different theologies. . . .

Werewolf Superstitions

The Werewolf superstition is exceedingly widespread; [German historian and folklorist W.] Hertz has collected examples of it from the most diverse countries. The person concerned was generously believed to have been seized by an irresistible impulse, a ravenous craving, to have changed their appearance and roamed through the fields devouring sheep and other animals or even human beings, especially children. As a rule the state was a temporary one, recurring at night, and there could be long lucid intervals. Spontaneous transformation into a wolf was as a rule achieved by the person either donning a wolf's skin or by his merely turning his own skin inside out. For he was supposed to wear a wolf's skin under his own, a belief which gave rise to horrible tortures in the Middle Ages, when suspected persons were hacked to pieces in the endeavour to find the hairy growth. Hair and Werewolf were closely associated ideas, as is illustrated by the Russian name for Werewolf, 'volkodlak' from *volk* = wolf, and *dlak* = hair. Werewolves could be recognized when in human form by having heavy eyebrows that met together, or by having hair on the palms of their hands. The sexual association of hair is of course well known. It was believed that the wolf's skin could be discarded, and if it was burnt the particular subject lost the power of transforming himself into a wolf; on the other hand, if one took away his human garment while he was in the wolf condition, he had to stay a wolf for ever. This last point is a familiar *motif* in mythology, for example, in the fairy tales of swan-maidens. The wolf's skin could be donned only when the person was naked. . . .

The popular idea about the reasons why anyone became a Werewolf bears a remarkable resemblance to those concerning other mythological creatures, *e.g.* swan-maidens, etc., and it would lead us too far from our theme to enter on a full explanation of them here. The most prominent feature is the belief that such a transformation can come about in two quite different ways according as the person in question brought it about voluntarily or was forced into it against his will. In the latter contingency there were three causes: Fate, magic and sin; with the first two of these it was his misfortune, with the third his fault. A saint or ecclesiastic could condemn a wicked person to become a Werewolf, usually for a term of years, a sentence very like excommunication; again a witch or devil could bring it about, with or without the person's consent. Thus, sinful women were turned into wolves for a space of years, usually seven. To transmogrify someone into a Werewolf a hide or a girdle of human skin was necessary, but sometimes a plain ring would suffice. The spell, particularly when due to fate, could be broken in various ways, the usual methods being to call him by his baptismal name, to tell him that he was a Werewolf, *i.e.* to reproach him with being one, or merely to recognize him; a peculiarly appropriate measure, which must remind us of the method of 'releasing' a Vampire by eating his flesh, was to make three sharp stabs at his forehead.

When the mediæval scholastic theologians got to work on the problem they accepted the facts, but, whereas some were of opinion that the animal transformation really happened, others maintained that it was merely a deception of the devil's. All agreed, however, that the proper treatment of the condition was to destroy, preferably to burn, the unfortunate object. . . .

Psychological Reasons Behind Superstitions

We have now to consider the psychological meaning of the superstitious belief in Werewolves. The three essential constituents of the belief are, as we have seen, the ideas of animal transformation, of ravenous cannibalism and of nocturnal wandering. I shall argue that the most important contributions to these three elements were furnished by the experiences of anxiety dreams of a kind that represent only a slight elaboration of the typical Nightmare. In this connection [noted German psychologist W.] Wundt . . . cautiously remarks:

'It is possible that the Werewolf myth similarly contains effects of nightmares and allied anxiety dreams, notably in the idea that the transformation of a human being into a wolf was supposed to have been brought about by encircling the body with a girdle of wolf-skin, as also in the feelings of terror experienced by the victim who was overpowered by the Werewolf; it is to be noted further how the Werewolf and Vampire legends have intermingled in many parts of the world. The ideas of animal transformation, which occur both in dreams and in mental disturbances, also play their part here.'

The Werewolf's Origin in Dream Experiences

In the first place, the very fact that the phenomena in question were supposed to occur at night, and during the sleep of the victims, should lead one to suspect an origin in dream experiences. In the second place, the extraordinary intermingling and interchangeability of the Werewolf with the Incubus and Vampire beliefs, both of which we have shown to have probably been derived in the main from dream experiences, would strongly suggest a similar origin here also. In the third place, the three elements enumerated above bear specially close relations to the *motifs* of anxiety dreams.

It is interesting that any two of these three elements can occur together without the third: (1) Nocturnal wandering and animal transformation we are already familiar with in the case of the Vampire. (2) Animal transformation and cannibalistic lust are found together with the rye-wolf (*Roggenwolf*). He does not wander by night, it is true, but it is to be noted that his depredations take place during the (mid-day) sleep of the victims. (3) Nocturnal wandering and cannibalistic lust often occur together apart from the idea of animal transformation. . . .

Dreams, Sleepwalking, and Repressed Desires

We have previously traced the belief in *animal transformation* largely to dream experiences.

The belief in *night wandering*, *i.e.* the belief that a given person can be in two places at the same time, certainly originates, as does actual somnambulism, also from dream experiences, for its development can still be observed among savages. It was believed that the real body of the Werewolf lay asleep in bed while his spirit roved the woods in the form of a wolf; further, when the wolf was wounded, corresponding wounds were to be found on the human body that remained at home. The similarity with the ideas of savages on dreams, . . . is plain enough. There are various sources for these travelling dreams, since they can symbolize a considerable number of repressed wishes: the wish for freedom from compulsion, one which the idea of a wolf very well represents, and especially for independence from the father; the wish for heightened potency, symbolized by swift movement, etc. The ultimate source of interest in movement is to be sought in the sexual component of agreeable sensations of this kind experienced by the infant.

Werewolves Symbolize Sadistic Tendencies

The third element would in psycho-analytical terminology be described as an oral-sadistic or cannibalistic impulse.

That the lust for tearing and devouring flesh is oral-sadistic in nature is evident to anyone acquainted with sexual pathology, and has, indeed, been pointed out by various other writers. The wolf symbolism is specially well suited to represent this, and the effect is heightened by the fact that Werewolves were supposed to be even more savage than other wolves. Sadistic tendencies prove in analysis to be derived from two sources. On the one hand we have the primary sadistic erotism of the young child, beginning with the oral-sadistic attitude towards the mother's breast—in which connection we recall the essentially dental nature of the wolf sadism—and revealing itself most typically in the classical belief in the sadistic conception of parental coitus. On the other hand there is the jealous hostility—later sexualized—against the parent of the same sex, so that both sources of sadism are rooted in the Oedipus complex. It is perhaps not a matter of chance that hatred of the father was a striking characteristic in the actual cases of Lycanthropy, *i.e.* where people really imagined that they wandered about at night in the guise of wolves. The cannibalistic idea of devouring human flesh, so characteristic of the Werewolf superstition, is derived from both the sources just mentioned, *i.e.* the erotic and the hostile; in the unconscious, as we know well from psycho-analysis, there is for these different motives the wish to devour both the loved and the hated object.

These sadistic tendencies have, of course, many manifestations in waking life, but the majority of them, *e.g.*, those that lie behind certain neurotic symptoms, are veiled, and very seldom reach elsewhere the fierce intensity which is so frequently met with in certain types of anxiety dreams. This consideration would lead one to ascribe to such dreams a considerable part in generating beliefs founded on the sadistic tendency, though not such a predominant one as with the two other elements discussed above.

From this point of view it is not surprising to hear that the group of unconscious ideas that lies behind the belief in, and fear of, Werewolves occasionally bursts through into consciousness in a positive form, with the result that the person afflicted with the delusion of being a wolf indulges in corresponding behaviour. As early as in the second century a medical work, by Marcellus Sidetes, pointed out that Lycanthropy was a form of insanity. He says that men are most attacked with this madness in February, that they skulk in cemeteries and live alone like ravening wolves. Clinically they would be classified as cases of sadism, frequently combined with cannibalism and necrophilia; they may or may not be associated with an actual lycanthropic delusion, there being many authentic examples of both.

In this connection it is interesting to note that the ideas associated with that of wolves reveal how profoundly the people apprehend the essence of anti-social behaviour to be sadistic in nature.

Lycanthropy, the Wolf Madness

Adam Douglas

British historian Adam Douglas covers all aspects of the werewolf mystery in his book *The Beast Within,* from which the following essay is taken. In this rather lengthy piece, Douglas details the case studies of several individuals diagnosed with lycanthropy, or wolf madness. Although evidence describing werewolves and wolflike behaviors literally spans centuries, it has only been in the last twenty years that scientists and psychologists have gathered enough evidence to name lycanthropy as a viable clinical diagnosis for those suffering from this type of mental disorder. Still, Douglas points out, there are difficulties. Researchers have been unable to strictly define symptoms and behaviors that apply across the board to all patients suffering from the disorder. In clinical studies, there are individuals who possess some but not all of the defining characteristics. Those whose behavior and symptoms are outside the norm have needed extensive further study and testing, all of which suggests that the disease is more complex than at first thought. Douglas emphasizes that lycanthropy is a rare syndrome. As such, perhaps it cannot explain all of the eyewitness accounts reported throughout history. Still, the disorder has been legitimized, and although werewolves might exist in a very real way in the minds of those suffering from lycanthropy, the tales, mythologies, and superstitions that have grown up around them can be seen as generally fictional.

As the houselights dim, the cinema-goers take their seats, and a sense of hushed expectancy spreads through the auditorium. The film about to be shown could be any one of a number regularly made on the subject since the earliest days of cinema—the plot has been used often enough to have become almost set in stone. The innocent hero of the film begins by breaking with his usual routine, perhaps by wandering off the beaten track, visiting a strange new country, or simply entering a dark forest. Suddenly, in the first of several gasp-inducing moments of violent drama to come, he is attacked by an unknown and terrible creature. The audience watches intently as the hero recovers from the ferocity of this attack and tries to carry on as normal, oblivious to the implanted bacillus doing its destructive, invisible work within him. Tension slowly builds all the while, the dreadful time approaching as inevitably as the monthly reappearance of the full moon in the night sky, the signal for the cataclysmic eruption when the monstrous animal *alter ego* will burst forth in all its snarling, hackle-raising fury. After this explosive high point the film progresses more quickly, episodes of blood-bolstered ferocity alternating with scenes of bewilderment and pathos. Strange magical remedies are discussed, but all is futile—at last the terrible curse must be eradicated, at the sad cost of the life of the hero. The final shot lingers on the hero's body, returned to human shape, peaceful in death.

The audience files out of the cinema, sated. The film has offended none of its collective sensibilities. The film is supposed to be about lycanthropy—the transformation of a man into a wolf—but the film-makers have not been so naïve as to give a straightforward treatment of this peculiar metamorphosis. They are too aware that a real wolf looks disarmingly like some of the household pets on which many of their patrons lavish hours of care and attention, and are perhaps also conscious of growing public unease over the wolf's ecological plight. They know that they must play up the monstrous angle, and so their furry creations look only vaguely like real wolves as they snarl and stumble (almost always on two legs rather than four) to their inevitable end. They are also confident in the knowledge that their audience is, by and large, a sophisticated one—a group of people at least dimly aware of the subtle trickery of artful camera work, wise to the potential uses of rubber, yak hair, and skilful make-up, a group of willing accomplices to their own terrorizing. And finally, for all their careful tiptoeing around public sensibilities, the film-makers get away with presenting this lurid ninety-minute spectacle of blood, violence, and magic for the simple reason that for not more than a few deliciously fleeting moments of suspended disbelief does the audience really give credence to the existence of these wild, hirsute creatures. For sane, rational people living in the modern world, the werewolf is pure fiction.

For people whose sanity and rationality is in question, the matter is not so clear-cut. In 1988 a group of psychiatrists working for the regional prison service at Bordeaux, France, reported the case of a man they designated only as X. This man, twenty-eight years of age, was imprisoned after an incident in which a fifty-two-year-old man had been found dead in a car, his face showing signs of violent assault. Two other people were arrested on suspicion of involvement in his killing: a male accomplice of X's (referred to in the psychiatrists' report as Y), and a forty-four-year-old woman with whom X had been having a relationship for the past three years. Although the stories of the suspects conflicted to some degree, both the accomplice and the girlfriend agreed that the murder had resulted from a drunken meal all three had shared with the dead man, a meal which had got disastrously out of hand. The woman had stolen the dead man's wallet and demanded that he strip naked, threatening him and taunting him with accusations of homosexuality. According to both her and Y's version of events, X became fatally involved at this point, bludgeoning the man to the floor in a wild rage. Afterwards, they both maintained that X had cleaned up all traces of blood and burnt several papers which would have been incriminating evidence.

When setting out to discover any possible cause for this alleged outburst of murderous violence, the prison doctors found themselves confronted with the archetypal 'hard man', a muscular prisoner with deep-set, staring eyes, his face and heavily tattooed forearms extensively criss-crossed with a network of old scars. His explanation for his behaviour was as dramatic as his appearance, for X announced to his startled interrogators that he was, and had been for many years, a werewolf.

'It is blood trouble,' X told the doctors:

It is when I make myself bite like a rabid dog . . . as soon as I see blood I want to swallow it, to drink it . . . if I happen to cut myself, I drink my own blood . . . when I suffer an emotional shock, I feel myself undergoing a transformation, it's like my fingers are paralysed, I get a feeling like ants are crawling in the middle of my hand, I am no longer master of myself . . . I have the impression of becoming a wolf, I look at myself in the mirror, I see myself transforming, it's absolutely no longer my own face changing, the eyes stare out, wild-looking, the pupils dilate, I feel as if hairs are bristling out all over me, as if my teeth are growing longer, I feel myself in another skin, and afterwards I lose consciousness.

X believed that he was reincarnated from some former existence, and that he had other strange powers in addition to his ability to undergo these wolfish transformations, powers which he attributed to having sexual relations with older women. According to him, he had satisfied his enormous cravings for blood by visiting the quayside abattoirs [slaughterhouses] and drinking horses' blood while it was still warm, 'but it isn't animal blood I prefer, but human blood'.

Questioning of X's mistress suggested that this was not just a fantastical confession dreamt up on the spot to impress the prison psychiatrists. She told them that during their relationship X had often howled like a wolf at night and banged his head against the walls, and that he slept only lightly, like a wild animal. Throughout their relationship he had tormented her with his sadistic sexual desires, on many occasions biting her and becoming wildly excited at the sight of her blood. She had witnessed several of his transformation episodes, when he became extremely aggressive and violent, beating her and smashing up everything in the house. The doctors noticed also that X was receiving visits in prison from an old girlfriend. During these visits, she and X would exchange deep, bruising bites on the neck, becoming intensely excited while they did so.

Seeking the cause of these curious, apparently inhuman urges, the psychiatrists questioned X about his childhood. He told them that he was born in 1954, and that his father had killed his pregnant mother and two of his brothers. He had been in and out of many jobs, being a fireman, forger, medium, circus trapeze artist, and a member of the French Foreign Legion for ten years. He said that he had two daughters but unhappily both had been killed, the first by an incompetent doctor, the second squashed by a truck. He told the psychiatrists this tale without any significant variation several times, both verbally and in writing, and to different doctors at different times.

The only thing wrong with his account was that it was totally untrue. The doctors discovered that X had in fact been born in 1960, one of six children. While not as dramatic as having a murderer for a father, his early childhood had indeed been disturbed, his mother dying when he was only eighteen months old, and his father proving unable to raise him. Brought up from the age of five by his uncle and his late wife, X had become an aggressive and undisciplined child, forever running away from all forms of authority. He had suffered convulsions as a baby, was incontinent until the age of ten, and had been hospitalized many times, including a period at a psychiatric hospital. At the age of fourteen he entered the first of a number of homes for juvenile delinquents, and two years later was given a detailed psychiatric examination at the request of one of the many judges before whom he appeared. This examination revealed that X, although of average IQ, exhibited such instability of character that the psychiatrist could not foresee him ever holding down a lasting job. He suffered major anxiety and depressive episodes, he showed an inability to relate successfully either with members of his own family or with other children in the home (where he was nicknamed 'the house madman'), he had mutilated his own arms and chest on several occasions, and he led an intense fantasy life which spilled out in numerous romanticized stories.

His behaviour did not show much improvement on reaching adulthood. He fulfilled the juvenile court psychiatrist's prediction by proving unable to hold down a steady job, preferring to sponge off others or extort money from friends and lovers. He was married for a short time, but his wife became pregnant by someone he had known at the children's home, and they separated in 1983. In 1979 he had already been deemed unfit for national service, and when he later applied to join the Foreign Legion, he was turned down as unsuitable for entry into that legendary bolt-hole for misfits and desperadoes. He drank constantly, terrorized his neighbours, and was imprisoned a number of times on charges of theft, grievous bodily harm, fraudulent impersonation, and firearms violations.

The psychiatrists who examined him after the latest violent incident concentrated on the central question of whether X really believed his own story that he was a werewolf. They certainly had enough evidence that he had been in the habit of telling outrageous lies throughout his life: everyone—his immediate family, the authorities at the children's home, his frightened friends and neighbours—told them as much, and he himself had compounded that impression by giving them a completely fictitious autobiography while in custody. On the other hand, his former girlfriend's evidence suggested that his lycanthropic behaviour had been going on for some time, at least for the three years that she had shared his bed—evidence which implied that X's belief in his own story was strong enough to influence his behaviour quite profoundly. In seeking to understand their patient's condition, the psychiatrists revived the term *mythomanie*, coined by the French psychiatrist Dupré at the beginning of the century. By mythomania, Dupré meant 'the pathological tendency, more or less voluntary and conscious, to lie and to create imaginary stories'. He distinguished this from other psychological conditions in which the patient might tell lies or untruths, such as delirium and dementia, where the behaviour would be out of the patient's conscious control, as well as from cases where lying or distortion of the truth occurs for entirely understandable reasons. Dupré characterized the most clearly definable form of mythomania as being vain, malign, and perverse. The prison doctors thought that X's pathological fabulation was most clearly marked by vanity, as it appeared to lack a perverse intention to harm others directly.

As the representative of the modern werewolf, X indicates many important features of current strategies to distinguish sanity from insanity and truth from fiction. Doctors like the French prison psychiatrists weigh up the value of stories like his, armed with the clear knowledge that werewolves cannot exist. Not only do the doctors not believe in them, they can hardly bring themselves to accept that their patients believe in them, even when those patients show symptoms of gross mental disturbance. Yet still they recognize some connection between the patient in their care and the hairy, lumbering star of the classic werewolf films, and they continue to write articles with 'lycanthropy' in their titles for medical journals in which serious psychological debate takes place. In doing so, they are following an ancient tradition.

The meaning of the word lycanthropy—derived from the Greek words for wolf, *lykos*, and man, *anthropos*—is habitually extended by doctors to cover all cases of the condition in which the patient believes he or she has been transformed into an animal, although the rarely used 'therianthropy' is the more accurate term for non-specific animal transformation. Yet even in its most restricted meaning, where the belief referred to is of transformation into a wolf, lycanthropy is one of the oldest diagnoses in psychiatric literature. As early as the fifth century AD the condition was being described by doctors as one which resulted from disturbance of the melancholic humour. One of the most influential accounts came from the seventh-century physician Paulus Aegineta, who practised in Alexandria. He described patients suffering from 'melancholic lycanthropia' as being characteristically pallid. They were deficient in both tears and saliva and so suffered dry eyes and excessive thirst. Their legs were ulcerated from travelling about on all fours, and they suffered compulsions to wander about at night, particularly into cemeteries, where they could be found howling until dawn.

Aegineta's diagnosis depended on the humoural theory rooted in the writings of two of his compatriots and predecessors, often regarded as the founding fathers of medicine: Hippocrates (whose famous Oath doctors still swear) and Galen, who lived during the first century BC and second century AD respectively. As the Periodic Table at that stage had only four recognized 'elements'—earth, air, fire, and water—it was reasoned that the human body was also made of four elements: the bodily fluids, or 'humours'. These humours—melancholy (black bile), blood, choler (yellow bile), and phlegm—corresponded to the four elements and also, in some mysterious and largely unexplained way, to psychological states. This was an idea which was to remain important for an astonishing length of time, being the predominant theory in medical and psychiatric discourse for the next fifteen hundred or so years. The influence of its long reign is still felt today, in so far as 'melancholic', 'sanguine', 'choleric', and 'phlegmatic' are still recognizable descriptions of particular moods and characters. From the post-classic era right through to the Renaissance, diagnosis of a particular medical or psychiatric condition consisted of recognizing which of these four humours, or any combination of them, was being produced in excess, so that steps could be taken to remedy that imbalance. Paulus Aegineta's diagnosis placed the blame for lycanthropy squarely on an excess of melancholy or black bile, and most of the physicians who came across the syndrome after him agreed. Although the theory behind the medical practice now seems nonsensical and unscientific, his description of the syndrome itself is excellent evidence that, at an early date, people were exhibiting symptoms very similar to those of Monsieur X from Bordeaux.

Twentieth-century doctors have been much less willing to admit lycanthropy as a syndrome: that is, a particular, discrete concurrence of symptoms. Armed with what are felt to be more sophisticated explanations for abnormal behaviour, psychiatrists appear to have dispersed what lycanthropic patients they have under different diagnostic subheadings. Many authorities have noted a general decline in the numbers of patients presenting with animalistic symptoms of any kind, and in particular in the numbers of patients thinking themselves to be wolves. This is usually ascribed to the feeling that increasing industrialization has resulted in people living more and more apart from the animal world. In addition, the great decline in the wolf population, especially in North America and continental Europe, has inevitably meant that far fewer people have ever seen a wolf, let alone felt drawn to identify with one. Towards the latter part of the twentieth century a consensus seemed to have been reached among western psychiatrists which regarded lycanthropy as an outmoded or unnecessary diagnosis, the term being either omitted from psychiatric handbooks or simply described as extinct. Yet cases do still occur which Paulus Aegineta would certainly have recognized as belonging in his category of 'melancholic lycanthropia'.

In 1975, Doctors [Frida G.] Surawicz and [Richard] Banta reported two cases of lycanthropy, the first of which, the case of Mr H, a twenty-year-old Appalachian man, was apparently largely explicable through the patient's history of long and chronic abuse of a variety of drugs, including marijuana, amphetamines, psilocybin, and LSD. While serving in the US Army in Europe, Mr H had taken LSD during some time he had spent alone in the woods. He hallucinated that he was turning into a werewolf, and saw fur bristling out on his hands and felt it growing on his face. Once transformed, he was filled with an irresistible urge to chase, kill, and eat wild rabbits. Back at his Army base after two days, Mr H remained obsessed with the idea that he was a werewolf and that he had been made privy to satanic secrets. The sign 'feeding time' in the mess hall convinced him that the others knew he was a wolf. His delusion proved resistant to various remedial programmes, and he remained obsessed with ideas of diabolic possession, particularly after seeing the film *The Exorcist*.

If Mr H's grip on reality had been damaged by persistent drug abuse, so the second case of lycanthropy reported by Surawicz and Banta had a similarly concrete cause. The behaviour of Mr W, a thirty-seven-year-old farmer, had been seen to deteriorate over a period of time, as he gradually let his facial hair—or fur, as he preferred to call it—grow long. He took to sleeping in cemeteries, howling at the moon, and occasionally lying down in the road in the midst of traffic. He explained his bizarre behaviour by saying that he was transformed into a wolf, but doctors who examined him were more concerned with transformations of a neurological kind taking place in his brain. They were able to compare their results with tests Mr W had previously taken while in the United States Navy, at which time he had shown a normal and average IQ. Surawicz and Banta's tests showed his IQ to have slipped to levels of moderate mental retardation, and brain scans and a biopsy suggested that this was due to some slow-acting brain disease. His episodes of thinking himself a werewolf seemed to have occurred as a direct result of his brain deteriorating, and although these werewolf delusions were prevented with drugs, Mr W remained an outpatient with impaired function and little sign of spontaneous mental activity.

Two years after the reporting of the cases of Mr H and Mr W, another lycanthrope appeared in the medical literature: a forty-nine-year-old American woman who suffered lupine obsessions which culminated in the delusion of transformation into a wolf. During the twenty years of her marriage, she had been troubled by urges towards bestiality, lesbianism, and adultery, as well as by an obsession with wolves which led her to think and dream about them constantly. Eventually she acted on her impulses, tearing off her clothes at a family gathering, and adopting the mating position of a female wolf in front of her mother. The next day, after sexual intercourse with her husband, she spent two hours growling, scratching, and gnawing in bed. She told the doctors that she had been possessed by the devil during these episodes and become an animal. In a hospital, under a treatment programme combining drugs and psychotherapy, her delusions persisted for a few weeks and she was able to describe them in some detail: 'I am a wolf of the night: I am a wolf woman of the day . . . I have claws, teeth, fangs, hair . . . and anguish is my prey at night . . . the gnashing and snarling of teeth . . . powerless is my cause. I am what I am and will always roam the earth long after death . . . I will continue to search for perfection and salvation.' Her reflection, gazing back at her from the mirror, seemed to her to show 'the head of a wolf in place of a face on my own body—just a long-nosed wolf with teeth, groaning, snarling, growling . . . with fangs and claws, calling out "I am the devil." In her reflection she had seen a terrifying distinction between her eyes: 'one is frightened and the other is like the wolf—it is dark, deep, and full of evil, and full of revenge of the other eye. This creature of the dark wants to kill.' During these episodes, she was in a state of wild and tormented sexual arousal, and was observed by doctors and fellow-patients making unintelligible animalistic noises.

Her doctors concluded that their patient suffered from 'chronic pseudo-neurotic schizophrenia' and responded to the kind of treatment used in cases of acute schizophrenic psychosis. They emphasized the sexual nature of the case, and believed that the strong internal conflicts aroused by the woman's compulsive thoughts of illicit sexual activity were expressed in her werewolf delusions. Despite the different terminology used, and the doctors' post-Freudian awareness of suppressed sexual motivations, there is a clear line of descent from Aegineta's lycanthropes to this patient, if only in her obsessive talk of graveyards. Even after her final lycanthropic episode, which coincided with the full moon, she wrote down her determination to continue the search 'for [what] I lack . . . in my present marriage . . . my search for such a hairy creature. I will haunt the graveyards . . . for a tall, dark man that I intend to find.'

Other cases subsequently appeared in the medical literature under the heading 'lycanthropy', although no more werewolves were immediately reported. Typical was the case of a sixty-six-year-old widow visiting friends in Ireland, who had become aggressive towards some members of their family for no particular reason, and had behaved in an animalistic way. During these episodes she would drop onto all fours and bark like a dog. (Her symptoms are properly described as 'kynanthropic', from Greek *kynos*, dog.) In hospital she was able to recall these occasions, and said that she had thought she was a dog at the time. She said that the devil had done this to her, and that she had been very frightened that if she were left alone, he would come down and take complete control over her. Her delusions and aggressive behaviour left her after treatment with anti-depressants and a course of electroconvulsive therapy.

Yet even this weight of evidence that lycanthropy still ex-

ists, at least in the form of animalistic behaviour accompanied by the patient's belief that he or she has somehow become an animal, is not found convincing by everyone. Some
authorities place more emphasis on the unique, and very
specific, causes for the behaviour in the individual psychology of each patient. Such lycosceptics argue that allegedly animalistic symptoms occur in many psychological disorders,
and that lycanthropy cannot be regarded as a medical or psychological diagnosis. What is needed is a wider frame of reference which might suggest how commonly such symptoms
occur in a recognizably distinct cluster. Such an overview was
provided in the late 1980s by doctors working at McLean
Hospital in Massachusetts, using the medical records of
some five thousand psychotic patients who had been treated
at their 250-bed private hospital in suburban Boston. The
doctors at McLean Hospital decided to go back through their
case histories accumulated over the previous twelve years,
noting any cases where, although it had not been diagnosed
as such, lycanthropy seemed to have occurred. As a govern-
ing principle, they decided that they would distinguish lycanthropes from those other patients who exhibited various
animal behaviours (barking, howling, biting, scratching,
crawling on all fours, defecating on the floor, and so on), but
who never said that they did so because they were animals.
Only those patients who exhibited animalistic behaviour *and*
at some stage explicitly declared themselves to be an animal
were to be included in their series. Using these diagnostic criteria, the McLean Hospital doctors unearthed twelve cases of
lycanthropy from their records.

The animals involved in these twelve cases varied. Only
two of the patients could be described as true lycanthropes
in the pedantic sense of the word, imagining themselves to
be transformed into wolves. The therianthropic crawling,
growling, hooting, twitching, and barking behavior of the

others came from two patients who thought that they were dogs, two who thought themselves to be cats, and one who insisted that he was a Bengal tiger. Perhaps more surprisingly, other bestial *alter egos* included a bird, a gerbil, and a rabbit who hopped around the ward for a day. Two patients exhibited general behaviour sufficiently feral to be included in the survey, but did not specify which animal they believed themselves to be. Five–sixths of the patients were male, and the ages of the patients ranged within a comparatively narrow band between sixteen and thirty-seven, although these data may simply reflect the general make-up of the hospital population.

It cannot be said that the McLean Hospital survey demonstrates that lycanthropy as the psychiatrics understand it is very often a particularly strongly-held or intractable delusion. Confronted by doctors, the 'tiger' and 'rabbit' both admitted that their animalistic behaviour was under their voluntary control, while another patient only developed the delusion of being a wolf after smoking hashish during a manic episode. In all but one significant case, the lycanthropic episode lasted a short time, quickly remitting following either confrontation or antipsychotic drug treatments—the hashish-smoking werewolf held out longest at three weeks. This was certainly consistent with the generally speedy remissions in the other cases that had come to light since 1975, although Surawicz and Banta's Mr H might be regarded as an exception in this respect.

Anybody who hoped that Aegineta's fifth-century diagnosis of 'melancholic lycanthropia' would turn out to have survived into the twentieth century under another name, that it would prove to be strictly identical with some modern medical diagnostic entity, was destined to be disappointed by the McLean Hospital survey. The McLean doctors laid out their results in a table which listed summary details of their twelve cases, with a column devoted to a description of the diagnosis based on that made at the time by the case doctor. The doctors felt justified in updating the original diagnosis because the universally accepted terms used by American psychiatrists had changed during the twelve years covered by the survey. Diagnoses are customarily based on the American Psychiatric Association handbook, known as DSM. This handbook has been updated several times, and the latest edition the McLean doctors had available to them was the third, known as DSM-III, published in 1980. This handbook, which lists the symptoms which are generally recognized as indicating a particular diagnosis, is an impressive attempt by the psychiatric profession to impose something approaching scientific exactness on clinical judgements which are generally felt, at least by the layman, to be intuitive, subjective, and inexact. The results, however, occasionally reveal embarrassing evidence of just how quickly psychiatric fashions can change: DSM-II, for example, the edition used in the original diagnosis of those McLean Hospital patients admitted before 1980, includes 'homosexuality' as a psychiatric disorder. Nevertheless, DSM-III offered the best available guideline for generally accepted standards of clinical diagnoses, and the McLean doctors were obviously bound to use it. They also had the detailed original case-notes to work from in instances where they updated diagnoses previously made according to the criteria of DSM-II.

At first glance, the table produced a flurry of excitement, because eight of the twelve patients met DSM-III criteria for 'bipolar disorder' (probably better known by its older name of 'manic depression', a rather misleading cognomen for the condition in which sufferers may be either manic or depressed, or both alternately, but never both at the same time), six of them characterized as manic. But the doctors were quick to point out that this did not prove that there is a specific association between lycanthropy and bipolar disorder, chiefly because approximately half of all the patients admitted to the McLean Hospital with psychotic symptoms of any kind met the criteria for bipolar disorder, and a finding of eight bipolar cases out of twelve patients, therefore, could well be attributed to chance. Furthermore, in two bipolar cases the doctors felt that the episodes of lycanthropy could not be explained purely by reference to that disorder: one bipolar patient thought he was a wolf only after smoking hashish, while the belief of another patient that he was a rabbit was very short-lived and appeared to the doctors to be related to a 'factitious disorder with psychological features', a judgement which echoes that of the French doctors' finding of *mythomanie* in the case of their Monsieur X. The McLean doctors concluded that although lycanthropy was a syndrome which seemed to be very much alive and well in the twentieth century, it could not be regarded as a syndrome which was specific to any particular disorder.

However, another tentative conclusion which might have been drawn from the McLean data, that lycanthropy is always a short-lived syndrome, was dramatically shattered by the eighth case listed in their table. Some of the doctors involved in that paper returned to the subject in 1990 to give a fuller case history of this remarkable lycanthrope. The McLean Hospital Case 8 was an American male, born in 1964, who, despite eight years of virtually non-stop psychotherapy as well as treatment with a huge variety of psychotherapeutic drugs, continued to insist that he was a tiger. He dressed in tiger-striped clothes, allowed his fingernails to grow long, and cultivated long hair and bushy facial hair, all of which gave him a distinctly feline look. As a child he had been unsure what kind of cat he was, but as he grew older he had reached the conclusion that he must be a tiger because of his size, and he came to believe that his real parents must have been tigers, or else that he had a tiger ancestor. He was painfully aware of his physical dissimilarity to a tiger, and regarded his lack of a tail, stripes, or fur as a physical deformity. He spent a good deal of time visiting tigers in the zoo, petting them through the bars, collecting balls of their fur, and talking to them in cat language, which he believed he had been taught to speak at the age of eleven by Tiffany, the family cat.

As with several other modern lycanthropes, sexuality appeared to play a prominent role in Case 8's condition. From an early age he had been having close relationships with cats, hunting with them and sharing their kills of small animals, and eventually he began having sex with them on a serial monogamous basis. At the age of nineteen, he began the most intense relationship of all, with a tigress named Dolly who lived at the local zoo. Naturally he was unable to consummate this relationship, but during one of his four psychiatric hospitalizations he developed the fantasy that Dolly had managed to escape from the zoo and was visiting him in the early morning, slipping into his shower to have sex with him. He believed that she became pregnant, but that the cubs were stillborn and she stopped coming to the hospital. Dolly was eventually sold to a zoo in Asia, which caused him such intolerable grief that he attempted to hang himself.

Perhaps unsurprisingly, Case 8 had a deeply disturbed background and family history. Both his paternal grandfather and first cousin had committed suicide and two of his aunts had died in psychiatric hospitals, their conditions undiagnosed. Of his immediate family, he was closest to his two older sisters, both of whom suffered from very severe early-onset Crohn's disease (inflammation, thickening and ulceration of the intestine). He regarded his parents disdainfully as eccentric, inconsistent, and limited in intelligence. In his early infancy, his depressed mother had taken to her bed for long periods, allegedly because of her menopause. To keep him out of harm's way, his parents had often simply tied him to a tree alongside the family dog. He recollected that it was on these occasions he first began to behave like an animal. Later, when he developed his relationship with Tiffany, the feline who taught him 'cat language', he idealized her as a better parent than the emotionally unstable couple whose fights and threats of divorce upset him so much throughout his youth. When asked about the qualities of cats, it was noticeable that he mentioned that cats are excellent parents, unlike humans.

In many respects Case 8 was able to lead a normal life. Apart from his lycanthropic delusion, his thought processes and perception were reported to be usually logical. Although he suffered recurrences of major depression and some hallucinations during his psychotic episodes, at other times he was able to combine his human and feline activities quite successfully, something which he said encouraged Tiffany. He had been involved in a number of successful sexual relationships with women, although he claimed to prefer cats, and the doctors noted that his infatuation with Dolly had begun immediately after the breakup of his closest human sexual relationship. Drug treatments proved effective in controlling his major depressions, and he was able to return to his steady job as a research scientist, and to the apartment he shared with two friends and a cat. And yet his central belief that he was a cat proved entirely intractable to any treatment.

Obviously the psychological significance of his peculiar upbringing is crucial to an understanding of Case 8's lycanthropy. A case with some similar features was reported by the child psychologist Bruno Bettelheim, in which a child suffering from poor parenting grew to identify with the family dog. In that case the mother had apparently shown more affection for her dogs than for her daughter, saying that the thought of living with her daughter 'made her so sick that she couldn't sleep or eat'. She had beaten the child severely and locked her in cupboards, and, whenever she could, had sent the child off to foster parents. Ironically, her most heartfelt complaint about her own childhood was that her mother treated her 'like a trained dog'. Around the age of two, the girl began to act like a dog. She crawled around on all fours, shared the dog's food, and chewed up furniture and rugs. Taken into care at the age of four because of parental neglect, she identified only with the dog at the specialized foster home in which she was placed. She ate dog biscuits, bit and scratched anyone who interfered with her, and carried objects around in her mouth, just like a puppy. However, the important difference between hers and Case 8's history is, once again, the remarkable endurance of Case 8's delusion. Taken from her mother and given appropriate psychotherapy, Bettelheim's dog-girl soon abandoned her kynanthropic behaviour—indeed for a while she became deeply agitated whenever she saw a dog. What her prompt recovery of human faculties suggests is that, given extreme circumstances, anyone may temporarily behave like an animal, but that there may be some extra factor which pushes people, like Case 8 one step further into long-term delusion.

Most contemporary psychiatrists—adherents of the so-called medical model of mental illness—argue that this is true in all cases, that while the particular nature of a psychosis may be explained by the patient's individual circumstances, not all people who suffer similar deprivation go on to develop mental illness. A possible medical explanation for Case 8's persistent lycanthropy was indicated by an electroencephalograph reading which suggested that he was suffering from a form of epilepsy. He had already reported visual distortions and episodes of *déjà vu* which had occurred from the age of seventeen onwards, and, taken with EEG reading, this accorded with a diagnosis of temporal lobe epilepsy. The McLean Hospital doctors pointed to a study which estimated an incidence of persistent psychosis in over 10 per cent of cases of temporal lobe epilepsy. The same source cited a number of studies which pointed to the existence of a particular psychosis among such patients, a psychosis characterized by a high incidence of delusional states which would otherwise be regarded as rare. Such patients will appear otherwise normal, but will be preoccupied with old delusional ideas. The McLean Hospital doctors pointed out the similarities between this psychosis and the history of their Case 8.

This intriguing modern medical evidence, when taken as a whole, shows clearly that lycanthropy is a syndrome, albeit rare, which turns up on a regular basis. In western psychiatric hospitals it is usually found to be short-lived, but in combination with certain other catalysts may persist for some considerable time, and can sometimes even resist all the best efforts of modern psychiatrists, using their twin weapons of psychotherapy and drugs, to wipe it out. It is reasonable to assume that in less technological societies, where psychology and pharmacology are not employed to the same ends, a proportionally greater number of lycanthropes will be able to persist in their delusional state (although this begs the question whether the modern patients would have imagined themselves to be werewolves if they had not a pre-existing cultural figure to emulate).

As a group of symptoms, it is obvious that lycanthropy cannot be linked with any one particular diagnostic category of mental illness, and a definitive inquiry into its causes looks like a hopeless task. However, a number of areas of possible inquiry are suggested by the collected case histories. One noticeable feature, both of the French case of Monsieur X and of the American Case 8, is the evidence of distressing emotional deprivation in childhood, in the latter case particularly associated with the idea that someone treated like an animal may eventually begin to behave like one. Bettelheim's dog-girl seems to back up this idea, and there is a great deal of historical evidence which can be put forward in favour of this thesis, although, of course, many people who are treated badly in childhood do not subsequently develop such bizarre delusions. They may be tied up like an animal as a baby, without behaving like one later in life.

Perhaps a more fruitful initial line of inquiry is suggested by the relationship between the lycanthropic episodes and the patients' expressions of their own sexuality. The wolf-woman tearing off her clothes and crouching down before her mother offers the most startling evidence of this relationship. In her case, it is clear that the adoption of the werewolf *alter ego* supplied her with an outlet for the expression of 'bestial' urges which both she and her immediate social circle would have much preferred to keep submerged. Even after lycanthropic delusion had faded away, she was able to retain the important idea that the delusion had revealed a hidden truth, that she was searching for some kind of sexual fulfillment she had yet to find in her married life. Case 8, too, expressed his sexuality through his lycanthropic episodes—indeed, of all modern lycanthropes, he is the only one who is reported actually to have committed bestiality in the old-fashioned or theological sense, by engaging in sexual activity with an animal. Even here, though, the coincidence between the end of one of his human sexual relationships and the beginning of his infatuation with the zoo tigress suggests that his relationships with animals were, in some sense of which he himself was unaware, a replacement or substitute for relationships with humans. In the same way that he turned to and idealized the cat Tiffany as a parent after the failure of his disastrous early upbringing, so he idealized the tigress Dolly after the failure of one of his adult attempts at normal human sexual relations. Monsieur X's bestial urges, on the other hand, his sadistic sexual practices and blood-fetishism, are more of a piece with his self-image as a hard man, seeking to intimidate even the prison doctors with his deep, staring eyes, an observation reinforced by the French doctor who mentioned vanity as the abiding characteristic of his mythomania.

Such psychosexual analyses can only tell part of the story. Evidence of organic disease affecting the brains of these lycanthropes would provide a much more specific aetiology for the syndrome, and there is a tantalizing glimpse of such evidence in at least two of these cases. Case 8's temporal lobe epilepsy was seen by his doctors as a factor possibly explaining the persistence of his delusion, while poor Mr W was described by the neurosurgeon who performed a biopsy on him as having a 'walnut' brain, the outer layer, or cerebellum, showing signs of distortion and degeneracy. His werewolf delusions seem only to have occurred during the period when his brain was undergoing this slow deterioration. Apart from Case 8, two other McLean patients showed neurological abnormalities, but these were only slight and were felt to be unremarkable by the doctors. Apart from disease, the other agent which might produce changes in the brain sufficient to account for lycanthropy would be a drug of some kind. Mr H's werewolfism was accounted for by his doctors as resulting from chronic abuse of a wide variety of drugs, together with a particular incident of LSD use, and one of the McLean lycanthropes developed his werewolf delusions after smoking hashish while in a manic state.

Two distinct werewolves stalk the dark forests of the

modern psyche: the cinematic and the psychiatric. On a superficial level, the differences between them are readily apparent. One dwells in a purely imaginary world where internal change is expressed through external metamorphosis, where the cycle of the moon brings forth yellow eyes and snarling fangs, where a single bite is fatal, where the sad but effective remedy of the silver bullet will stop the beast; the few examples of the other have been co-opted to a purely factual world of science and medicine, where learned papers give sophisticated analyses of psychological trauma and neurological damage. The cinematic werewolves live on as a vivid image of what Plato called the beast within us, man's individual capacity for slaughter and rapine, although it is an image that usually belongs only to the past, a Hollywood Gothic of shambling monsters and panicky villagers, a world at once melodramatic, vaguely laughable, and safely distanced from our everyday lives. The psychiatric werewolf lives on in sadder isolation, surrounded by well-meaning doctors who carefully probe the workings of his mind in the hope of uncovering clues to this and greater mysteries. Subjected to a blizzard of questions about his childhood, targeted by a hopeful fusillade of pharmaceutical silver bullets (over an eight-year period Case 8 alone was prescribed an unstated number of tricyclic antidepressants, trazodone, isocarboxazid, lithium carbonate, carbamazepine, valproate, and haloperidol), occasionally even subjected to the dubious last resort of electroconvulsive therapy, the psychiatric werewolf, like his cousin on the silver screen, is kept at a discreet distance from respectable society. When his delusions and deceptions are catalogued even by the most sympathetic, non-judgmental observer, he is always in danger of arousing incomprehension and ridicule only slightly tinged with pity, of being casually dismissed with the colloquialism 'barking mad'.

Mental Illness as an Explanation for Werewolves: Two Case Studies

Frida G. Surawicz and Richard Banta

Dr. Frida G. Surawicz is an established authority on diseases of the mind. As an associate professor of psychiatry at the University of Kentucky Medical College, as well as the chief of psychiatry for the Veterans Administration Hospital in Lexington, Kentucky, Surawicz worked closely with her colleague Dr. Richard Banta, a resident at the University of Kentucky Medical College, to treat the two case studies of lycanthropy evaluated in this viewpoint. Surawicz and Banta provide a brief overview of the various historical perspectives on lycanthropy, as well as traditional treatments for lycanthropes prior to the twentieth century. They then present the well-known cases of Mr. H. and Mr. W. Both men suffer from various psychoses including schizophrenia, but the

Frida G. Surawicz and Richard Banta, "Lycanthropy Revisited," *Vampires, Werewolves and Demons: Twentieth Century Reports in the Psychiatric Literature*, edited by Richard Noll. New York: Brunner/Mazel, 1992. Copyright © 1992 by Richard Noll. Reproduced by permission of Routledge/Taylor & Francis Books, Inc.

causes, symptoms, and final diagnoses of each disorder differ. The doctors conclude that lycanthropy—or the delusion that one is a werewolf—can be considered a unique symptom of some contemporary psychiatric disorders, making a strong case for the fact that werewolves simply do not exist outside of delusional imaginings by the mentally ill.

Most contemporary textbooks, with the exception of the *American Handbook of Psychiatry*, do not mention the term lycanthropy—the delusion of being changed into a wolf. Recently [late 1960s to early 1970s], two patients with symptoms of this disorder were admitted and studied on an inpatient service. Their cases are reported here because of the unusual symptomatology of this allegedly extinct condition.

The literature on lycanthropy is extensive and includes publications from ancient as well as modern times [up through the twentieth century]. It is widespread across the world. The near extinction of wolves in Western Europe and most of America may well have diminished the occurrence of lycanthropy in the Western World but the condition continues to exist in a modified form in China, India, Indonesia, Assam, Malaysia, and in many African countries. In these countries, the delusions include transformation into other ferocious animals, such as hyenas, tigers, crocodiles, and wolves.

The definition of lycanthropy through the ages is fairly universal, namely that once a man is changed into a wolf, he acquires its characteristics, roaming around at night, howling in cemeteries and attacking man or beast in search of raw flesh. However, there have always been two interpretations of this condition, often diametrically opposed.

The religious interpretation, based on mythology and superstition, sees the metamorphosis of man into wolf either as a divine punishment or as the outcome of a pact with the devil. This interpretation was first recorded in Greek mythology, when Lycaon, a tyrant in Arcadia, in order to test Zeus, secretly fed him the flesh of a slayed Molossian. Zeus became outraged, destroyed Lycaon's palace and transformed him into a howling wolf. Medieval and Renaissance theologians thought that werewolfism could be caused by the evil eye or by satanic ointments. Jean Bodin, a sixteenth century French physician, states that ". . . the devil can really and materially metamorphose the body of a man into that of an animal and thereby cause the sickness". In the twentieth century, Montague Summers believes firmly in werewolfism, and traces it back to an ancient cult connected with the Baal religion and probably imported by a Phoenician race in the former Arcadia in Greece, where wolves and the devil presumably were worshipped in high places and received human sacrifices.

In contrast, scientists and physicians from antiquity on have seen lycanthropy as a form of disease, either a type of melancholia with delirium, or drug induced. . . .

Peter Thyraeus explained the metamorphosis of man into wolf in three ways—it can be caused by hallucinations, or an animal form can be superimposed upon the human form, or a person can be cast into a slumber or trance by the devil, whereupon the astral body is clothed with an animal form. In contrast to these ambiguous positions, Donato Antonio Altomari, a physician in sixteenth century Naples, wrote that lycanthropy is indeed a disease predominantly occurring in February, characterized by excessive thirst and complete loss of memory of the attacks after recovery. Jean de Sponde believed that lycanthropy can be caused by noxious herbs which can drive man mad and affect his judgment and reason. He felt, however, that the devil will employ potions and unguents that have no power within themselves to affect the metamorphosis of man into wolf. This position was also held by Sieur de Beauvoys de Chauvincourt, who subscribed to the belief that drugs and toxic substances were involved to help the devil create a spell, deceiving both the sorcerer and those who saw him. In other words, under the influence of drugs, a person may hallucinate werewolves or see himself as a werewolf. . . .

In the twentieth century yet another explanation is offered by psychoanalysts who see lycanthropy as a proper vehicle for sexual, sadistic, cannibalistic and necrophilic instincts, split off from the ego on an animal level, and thereby immune from guilt.

The balance between these two different interpretations, religious-superstitious *versus* medical, has frequently been dominated by the first one, especially in Europe in the late Middle Ages and the sixteenth and seventeenth centuries, when lycanthropy was widespread and sometimes epidemic. With the prevalent religious belief that the disorder was a brand of sorcery and evidence of a pact with the devil, thousands of people were executed as werewolves. Despite these executions, the medical profession, as indicated above, increasingly emphasized the disease aspect and therefore treatment or incarceration into mental institutions occurred.

The clinical picture of the lycanthropes show an amazing consistency as ". . . pale, their vision is feeble, their eyes dry, tongue very dry, and the flow of saliva is stopped, but they are thirsty and their legs have incurable ulcerations from frequent falls". The treatment included exorcism as well as the traditional treatment for patients suffering from melancholia, which used to be a broad diagnostic term. This treatment began with bloodletting to the point of fainting, whereupon the patient was treated with a wholesome diet and baths. He was subsequently purged with colocynth, dodder of thyme, aloe, wormwood, acrid vinegar, and quills. In chronic cases, vomiting was induced with hellebore. The patient also obtained sedatives and his nostrils were rubbed with opium.

Mr. H., a 20-year-old single, unemployed white male from Appalachia, was admitted with a history of long and chronic drug abuse, including marijuana, amphetamines, psilocybin and LSD. His present sickness was precipitated by LSD and strychnine taken while he was in Europe with the United States Army ten months previously. He was out in the woods while he ingested the LSD, and felt himself slowly turning into a werewolf, seeing fur growing on his hands and feeling it grow on his face. He experienced a sudden uncontrollable urge to chase and devour live rabbits. He also felt that he had obtained horrible insight into the devil's world. After having been in this condition for two days, he rejoined his Army post but remained convinced that he was a werewolf. Looking for clues, he believed that the mess hall sign "feeding time" proved that other people knew that he was a wolf. He was sent to a psychiatrist who treated him with chlorpromazine [thorazine] for a few months. Six months thereafter he was returned to the United States on medical evacuation status to a drug program, where he was observed for a few weeks with a diagnosis of "drug abuse-amphetamines". During the next few months, the patient quit all drugs except marijuana, but continued to be preoccupied with the werewolf transformation. He felt worse after he saw the movie "The Exorcist" two weeks prior to admission.

The background history reveals that the patient's father left home during Mr. H.'s infancy and denied his paternity of the patient, but not that of his two older brothers. The patient felt that the father did this to maintain credibility with his mistress, whom he subsequently married. His first stepfather with whom he was very close, died in his presence, when he was seven. He lost his second stepfather through divorce in his early teens. The patient was very close to his mother. There is a family history suggestive of mental disease, and an older brother and a maternal cousin were denied admission to the Army because they were "weird and nervous".

The patient was sociable as a child. He started experimenting with hallucinogenic drugs in junior high. While in high school, he became interested in the occult and identified with a male priest who claimed to be a satanist. After high school the patient joined the Army where his drug use was intensified. Following his discharge from the Army after fourteen months he returned home and has been restless, hostile, agitated, anhedonic, socially withdrawn, and unable to maintain steady work. . . .

On admission the patient presented as a tense and suspicious young man who felt that the staff members might be possessed by or be tools of the devil. He had paranoid delusions, feeling that the devil at the end of each performance of "The Exorcist" goes out of the screen and possesses one of the movie goers. He had auditory hallucinations, hearing his thoughts aloud or his name being called, as well as visual hallucinations, during which he saw goats and black mass paraphernalia on the floor. When he looked in a mirror he occasionally saw a devil's claw over his eyes. He also believed that his thoughts were broadcast, and that the devil inserted thoughts into his mind and enabled him to read minds. He had unusual powers and felt that he could stare down dogs with his demoniacal gaze. He felt that the doctors put drugs in the patients' food to make them crazy. He showed marked ambivalence, seeking out doctors for long conversations, while at the same time expressing his fear of them. His affect was inappropriate and he would appear angry for no obvious reason, or giggle while discussing his stepfather's sudden death. . . . He attributed a shooting pain from the neck through the arms as a sign of possession. The patient gave a history of heavy and multiple drug use including LSD, amphetamines, mescaline, psilocybin, heroin and marijuana until his bad trip ten months ago, when he stopped taking LSD but continued to take amphetamines and marijuana. Since his discharge from the Army he continues to smoke marijuana regularly but has not taken any other drugs.

The MMPI [Minnesota Multiphasic Personality Inventory] was interpreted as ". . . compatible with an acute schizophrenic or toxic psychosis characterized by anxiety, obsessional thinking, agitation, religious delusions as well as bizarre sexual preoccupations and fears regarding homosexuality. Delusions of grandeur, ideas of reference and hallucinations may be present. A delusional system involving omnipotence, genius and special abilities may be present that could also be compatible with the profile of a male hysteric who has decompensated into a psychotic reaction."

The patient was treated . . . and showed gradual improvement. At the time of his discharge thirty-two days after admission, he had dropped the belief that he was a werewolf or that he was possessed and displayed no other overt psychotic determinants.

The patient was referred to an outpatient clinic near his hometown, two hundred miles from this hospital. He was seen for an interview at that clinic two weeks after his discharge and appeared polite but guarded, was preoccupied with satanism and had stopped his medications because they made him feel uneasy. No further contact was established with this patient, and it was thought by the staff that he perhaps felt threatened by the clinic. Attempts to call him for further visits failed.

Mr. W. is a 37-year-old single male farmer from Appalachia. At the time of his service in the United States Navy he had a normal and average IQ. Since his discharge after four years of service he has progressively and insidiously failed to function both as a farmer and in his daily activities. He has episodically behaved in a bizarre fashion, allowing his facial hair to grow, pretending that it was fur, sleeping in cemeteries and occasionally lying down on the highway in front of oncoming vehicles. There is also a history of the patient howling at the moon. Following two of these occasions, he was admitted to a psychiatric hospital. On the first admission he was given a diagnosis of "psychosis with mental deficiency", and marked deterioration of higher cortical functions was noted. During his second hospitalization, he was diagnosed as suffering from chronic undifferentiated schizophrenia, based on his bizarre behaviour since delusions or hallucinations could not be elicited while he was in hospital. During his third hospitalization, one year after his second hospitalization, the patient explained his bizarre behaviour by saying that he was transformed into a werewolf.

The mental status examination showed a patient who was tidy yet dirty and sat in a slumped position. His facial expression was blank and he showed paucity of motor activity. He did not display any concern about his hospitalization and his affect was flat. His speech was slow, but in general logical and coherent, with impoverished thought processes. Although little rapport could be established, the patient was in general cooperative and compliant. On cognitive function testing he showed markedly impaired attention and concentration. His ability to calculate was severely impaired, recent memory was moderately impaired, and remote memory was spotty. The ability to make objective judgments and to abstract was adequate. On physical examination, soft neurological signs were found, including bilateral hyporeflexia of the triceps, a slow second phase of both knee jerks and a thick speech with regarded flow. The remainder of the neurological examination was negative and the family history was noncontributory and negative for neuropsychiatric problems. The patient's symptoms began after he was discharged from the Navy. The patient had a positive brain scan, static, in the region of the right frontal cortex. Skull X-rays showed a lucid area in the right frontal region. The cerebral arteriogram did not show a mass lesion in the brain. The pneumoencephalogram showed no evidence of dilation, but the third ventricle was somewhat atypical in appearance. No pathological changes could be identified. [Patient's brain appeared normal.]

Psychological testing showed ". . . a mental age on the Peabody Picture Vocabulary Test of eight years one month and ten years five months respectively, corresponding to an IQ score of 57 and 68. On the Shipley Hartford Scale his vocabulary mental age was eleven years, nine months, his abstract mental age was eight years, four months and his conceptual quotient was 70. There was a variation in the testing and his verbal functioning level was at best in a mild retardation range with an IQ between 52 and 67. Considering his figure drawings and the Shipley Hartford Conceptual Quotient his level of impairment was even greater, probably in the moderate mental retardation range with an IQ between 36 and 51 or lower. There seemed to be indication of brain damage. On a concrete level, his ability to comprehend was surprisingly almost adequate. He was not capable of any abstract reasoning and psychomotor retardation was pronounced. If care was taken to communicate with him, he could communicate on a simple concrete level.". . .

The patient was discharged with a diagnosis of chronic brain syndrome of undetermined etiology. His psychotic behaviour has been successfully controlled with [medication] and no further episodes of lycanthropy have been reported since his discharge one year ago, but he continues to be inactive, seldom reads, and on his last visit to the Outpatient Clinic it was noted that he offers little spontaneous conversation. He appears quiet and childlike, answering most questions with "yes", "no", or "I don't know", but he did not show any evidence of abnormal behaviour or psychosis. Lycanthropy, by its very definition, would appear to point to a severe type of depersonalization. Many medical treatises from the past have indeed suggested that it is a form of hysteria. The endemic occurrence of the disorder and its mystical superstitious content have been used as supporting arguments. Many contemporary psychiatrists, when faced with the description of the recorded cases of the sixteenth and seventeenth centuries, would undoubtedly focus on the severe withdrawal, bizarre behaviour and delusions, impaired impulse control, and habit deterioration to support a diagnosis of schizophrenia.

The two presented cases shared lycanthropy but had a different diagnosis. The first was complicated by the history of drug use but was diagnosed as paranoid schizophrenia, perhaps precipitated and facilitated by drugs. The second case represented a chronic brain syndrome with periodic psychotic flare-ups. The common denominator would appear to be an onset precipitated by changes in brain disease in the second. Depersonalization has of course been frequently described by contemporary hallucinogenic drug users. The occurrence of depersonalization in convulsive disorders has also been noted. Therefore, the authors propose that in both instances an altered state of consciousness existed. In the first case, this was brought on by LSD and strychnine and continued casual marijuana use. In the second it must be assumed that a chronic altered state of consciousness was caused by irreversible brain disease, although the periodicity of his psychosis, occurring during the full moon, remains, unexplained on an organic level.

Epilogue: Analyzing the Evidence

Lycanthropy I comprehend, for without transformation
Men become werewolves on any slight occasion.

—Lord Byron, *Don Juan*

D o creatures such as werewolves really exist? Or are they simply a fiction created by the human imagination as a way to deal with irrational fears? The evidence presented in this book suggests that there is no easy answer to this question. The answer to the mystery of the werewolf is not black and white, and the question of its existence cannot be answered with a simple *yes* or *no*.

Developing a Critical Perspective

Your job is to evaluate the evidence presented in this book and to question how the authors reached their conclusions. Then you can decide whether the evidence presented helps you to determine where you stand on the question of whether werewolves exist. In order to evaluate the evidence effectively, you must examine it from a critical perspective. This means that you will look carefully at an author's work, the evidence presented, the way he or she argues his or her points, and the final conclusions. You will do this by asking questions about the writing and by breaking the argument down into several parts. You can then look more closely at these parts in an effort to determine whether the author's claim is based on solid research and objective analysis or if it is simply based on assumptions and uninformed opinions. Finding out if the evidence the author presents is reli-

able will help you decide whether it is possible that werewolves exist.

Thinking critically about a subject, such as the existence
of werewolves, involves questioning and evaluating the
topic objectively. This means that you do not think about it
according to your feelings on the subject but rather by focusing only on the evidence and facts as they are presented,
how well they are presented, and whether they are reliable.
By carefully evaluating and questioning the evidence, it is
possible to arrive at some form of truth, or at least to find
an answer to your questions about werewolves. The ability
to think critically takes practice. This epilogue is designed to
introduce you to several critical-thinking strategies that will
enable you to effectively evaluate the authors' evidence and
arguments about whether werewolves are fact or fiction.

Critical-Thinking Strategies and Goals

Your first task is to evaluate whether the evidence is based
on accurate research and information (generally reliable) or
if it is based on uninformed opinions and personal feelings
(usually unreliable). Valid opinions may be informed
through research, experience, or specialized expertise in a
field. But opinions may also be uninformed, meaning that
they are not verifiable through experience or expertise but
exist simply because the author wishes to hold them for
convenience or because they correspond with his or her
own values and beliefs. Simply because evidence is presented to you in a convincing way does not mean it must be
accepted as fact.

To illustrate and practice the critical-thinking techniques
you will use in evaluating the evidence presented in this
book, we will examine two of the articles in the book. One
piece, "Twentieth-Century Werewolves" by Brad Steiger, contains evidence that supports the existence of werewolves. The

other piece, "Rabies Epidemics Explain Werewolf Sightings" by Ian Woodward, presents evidence arguing against the existence of werewolves. The critical-thinking process is broken down into five steps. These steps will explain in detail what is involved in working through the strategy and demonstrate how to apply the strategy.

Step 1: Examining the Author's Credentials and Background

The first step in evaluating the evidence by Steiger and Woodward is to examine their credentials, or their background and experience. What qualifications do they possess that make it important for you to consider their claims and evidence? Answering this question is important for a couple of reasons. In order to form a solid conclusion of your own about whether werewolves exist, you want to have the best evidence at your disposal. The best evidence is most likely presented by authors who have done adequate research on the topic, who themselves demonstrate an ability to think critically about the issue, and who perhaps have some expertise in the study of werewolves that goes beyond their opinions and beliefs. Evidence presented by authors with these qualifications is generally considered more valuable and worthy of consideration.

However, even these qualifications do not make the evidence presented either for or against the existence of werewolves absolutely certain. This leads us to the other important reason for examining an author's credentials. The fact is, even experts can be wrong, or later proven to have been wrong, based on newer research. Experts hundreds of years ago in Spain believed the world was absolutely flat based on evidence that was reasonable and available to them at the time; however, Christopher Columbus' heroic ocean voyage proved them wrong. This does not mean that the experts of

Columbus's time were ignorant or deliberately misleading people; rather, they formulated their opinions based on the information available to them. It took someone with an altogether different hypothesis, or idea, to do additional research. This research introduced new facts and changed existing beliefs. Similarly, you might need to determine if the information these authors are providing to you is correct and has not been proven wrong by new research in the field of werewolf studies. If they are truly experts in their field, they will take very seriously their responsibility to present the most up-to-date research on the topic.

With this in mind, what can you tell about Woodward and Steiger and whether the evidence they present regarding the existence of werewolves is worth considering? What do their backgrounds and experience tell you about the potential reliability of their arguments?

In the biographical introduction to Steiger's piece, you are told that he is considered one of the most well known authorities on UFOs and aspects of the paranormal, including human transformation. He is a well-respected and published author of books in his field of research. His article is taken from his book *The Werewolf Book*, which is intended to be an encyclopedic look at the werewolf in history, society, literature, art, film, and culture. Obviously, to create a book with such a vast scope, Steiger had to do a great deal of research on werewolves. You might be inclined to accept him as an expert based on the fact that he has researched and published previously, though this does not mean that his research is necessarily well done or even accurate. He simply meets some of the important professional criteria (we will look more closely at the ways in which these two authors conduct their research and the evidence they use in Step 3). In addition to his writing and research experience, Steiger presents evidence for twentieth-century werewolves, namely that the word *werewolf* translates from the old Norse word for what we know as a serial killer, which lends some credibility to his assertion that modern-day serial killers can be viewed as werewolves. It also points to the importance of a thorough examination of details surrounding a topic (such as the meaning of a particular word) that could lead to evidence that will strengthen one's argument. Steiger's credentials indicate that his work is worthy of consideration.

The credentials of the other author, Ian Woodward, are less well known. Intensive biographical research on Woodward yields little information about his background and experience, though his name is known among those interested in the occult and paranormal for his book *The Werewolf Delusion*, from which "Rabies Epidemics Explain Werewolf Sightings" is taken. Woodward's book remains one of the top resources on the subject of werewolves for its clear writing and careful analysis of the topic. Not all of the books written on this topic are of such high quality. However, the fact that little is known about Woodward's expertise is problematic as it relates to this step in your analysis. Should you disregard his work simply because you cannot verify his practices and methodologies? Not necessarily. The quality of his work speaks where a lack of biographical information cannot. In this situation, you will have to reserve judgment about the author of the work and look solely at the work itself with the following question in mind: Can it stand alone as a viable piece of evidence even in the absence of biographical information about the author? In this case, the answer to this question is clearly "yes." Since it is your goal to examine the mystery of werewolves in relation to whether they are fact or fiction, the quality of Woodward's work speaks for itself as worthy of consideration, even without biographical information to speak to Woodward's credentials.

To practice the steps of developing a critical perspective in evaluating evidence, it is only necessary for us to examine the works of these two selected authors. However, you might be asked at some time to evaluate the work of several authors, selecting the best three pieces from six authors, for example. In this situation, it becomes even more important for you to examine the background and credentials of the authors you select. If you must choose the best evidence to support your argument, you will want it to come from the most reliable sources. We have discussed above the credentials of two of the twelve authors in this book and have found the credentials of Steiger to be impressive, but we have found little to recommend Woodward except the quality of his work. It is important to remember that if you are ever faced with a lack of information about an author's credentials, you should carefully consider whether the work might still be worth examining. If you were asked to choose between Steiger and Woodward based on credentials alone, you would likely choose Steiger's work over Woodward's. However, if you were asked to examine the works themselves in assisting you to determine which would be of the most expert value to your research, it is quite possible you would choose Woodward over Steiger. The author's possession of reliable credentials and expertise is quite possibly one of the most important things for you to look for when gathering evidence for a critical analysis; however, an absence of credentials does not immediately discredit the work. Solid credentials from the author do not necessarily mean the piece you are considering is the best one. The piece by the author with less expertise might be just as useful. These are important points to consider as you evaluate the work of the authors in this book.

Each author whose work is included in this book was chosen because he or she had something to offer on either side of the werewolf controversy. Remember, although credentials and experience are important, experts can sometimes be wrong or misinformed. Your job is to ask appropriate questions and think critically about the background of these experts.

Step 2: Determining the Author's Hypothesis

A hypothesis, or claim, is a statement concerning the main idea or point the author is trying to prove. Each author in this anthology presents evidence in support of one of two hypotheses: either that werewolves are fact or that werewolves are fiction. The facts and evidence used by the author to support his or her hypothesis can be tested for accuracy by further investigation or research.

How does the hypothesis work in practice? Based on experience or research, an author may hypothesize that werewolves are real. The author's questions or ideas about werewolves will guide his or her further research, looking for proof that they exist. The author will look for information that will support his or her hypothesis or answer his or her questions concerning werewolves. The author will then present this research in an effort to convince others that his or her hypothesis is correct. Others may disagree with the author's hypothesis that werewolves are real and go about using the same process to prove their hypotheses that werewolves do not exist.

It is important to identify the author's hypothesis so that you can determine whether the evidence the author uses to support it is strong and valid. In addition, if the author's hypothesis is not clear, you may conclude that the evidence he or she presents could also be weak or unclear. In this case, it may not be worthwhile for you to consider the article. The hypothesis should be clearly stated and provable. However, not all hypotheses are proven successfully. Although an author may make an attempt to prove the hypothesis, it can fail due to inadequate research or the author's reliance on his or her own opinions instead of reliable evidence.

The author's claim can usually be clearly stated in one or two sentences, but it may be longer and more complex in the piece you are examining. You need to try to synthesize the information the author is providing to you and restate the hypothesis clearly and simply in your own words. In some cases, the author may have more than one hypothesis in a single article. Each of these must be looked at separately in order to think critically about the entire article. Let's take a look at the hypotheses of Steiger and Woodward and discuss each one in detail.

Steiger's hypothesis: The close relationship between humans and wolves has existed since the dawn of time; as such, it is not difficult to see the ways in which the primal nature of the modern-day serial killer resembles that of the traditional werewolf. Steiger's piece is offered as one that provides evidence that werewolves exist. As mentioned above, Steiger examines the ways in which the relationship between wolves and humans has been closely intertwined throughout history. Steiger then presents well-known cases of modern-day serial killers, which he compares to the beastly rampages of eyewitness accounts of werewolves throughout history. He argues that the primitive beast, the wolf, lives within each of us and that only a very fine line separates our ability to behave as civilized human beings from our instincts to act out our basest animal desires. You will expect the evidence he provides to support his hypothesis.

Woodward's hypothesis: Eyewitness accounts of werewolves can be explained using scientific research that argues that those who were suspected of being werewolves really suffered from an acute case of rabies. Woodward's piece argues the opposite viewpoint, that werewolves do not exist. He hypothesizes that eyewitness accounts of werewolves can be explained by developing a greater understanding of the ways in which the rabies disease can be transmitted to and manifest itself in human beings, arguing that rabies epidemics follow a cyclical pattern of recurrence. Woodward's hypothesis concludes that werewolves exist only as human beings suffering from a disease with no known cause or cure at a time when superstition and occult practices were prevalent. Woodward's job is to convince you that his hypothesis is correct by providing evidence to support it.

Step 3: Evaluating the Evidence

Evidence is used to support the hypothesis of the author. Before we examine the types of evidence used by Steiger and Woodward in support of their claims for and against the existence of werewolves, it would be helpful to discuss briefly the different types of evidence available.[1] The authors in this anthology use the following types of evidence:

Personal experience. Evidence based on personal experience is not necessarily the most reliable form of evidence, but it is the most widely available. The problem with evidence based on personal experience is that it can be colored by subjectivity, or your feelings, values, and biases about a particular person, place, or thing.

Published reports. This form of evidence is usually one of the more reputable types, but it is still far from perfect. Evidence from published reports can be found from a wide variety of sources—basically anything in print, from encyclopedias to scholarly journals, from books to magazines. When considering evidence from published reports, quality is key. Research must be thorough and well documented. Statements must be clear and effective. Facts must not be confused with opinions.

Unpublished reports. Using this type of evidence is very risky since it is hard to confirm whether it is true. Unpublished reports may be gossipy in nature or may just be secondhand information that could have gotten skewed in the translation from person to person.

Eyewitness testimony. This type of evidence relies on the words of individuals who witnessed an event. It is usually considered highly reliable; however, it shares some of the same problems with personal experience and unpublished reports. Since it is based on an individual's perception and can be influenced by any number of factors, such as fear or environment, it is a subjective form of evidence. This means it is often colored by emotions or other factors that could cause the witness to perceive things inaccurately.

Expert opinion. Although not all opinions are considered to be objective, expert opinion is considered to be the most reliable form of evidence. Evidence based on the opinion of an expert may be informed by personal experience, but it is usually confirmed and validated based on research and professional expertise.

Experimental evidence. Experimental evidence can be produced in two locations. In the laboratory, the researcher can control and change the environmental and physical conditions of the experiment. Experiments in the field, although they have the benefit of occurring in a natural setting, can still be influenced by the researcher's presence or by conditions he or she introduces. When considering this type of evidence, you need to ask whether the results were influenced intentionally by the researcher to get the desired or hoped-for effect and what would have happened if the researcher had not interfered.

Formal observation. Like experimental evidence, there are two types of observational research methods. One form is called detached observation, in which the researcher is in the environment to observe and document what is happening. In participatory observation, the researcher actually participates in the event being observed. In both cases, the position of the researcher in relation to the events being observed can influence the final outcome. In both types of observation, the researcher may analyze and draw conclusions about his or her documentation.

Research review. This type of evidence is used by several of the authors in this book. It is less common since it is used only by writers who have access to a large body of research on a particular topic. This type of evidence involves reading all of the academic research on a topic. The author evaluates the findings and identifies the key points, recurring themes, or major controversies in the subject. He or she then summarizes all of the evidence for the reader. This approach to handling a large amount of evidence is effective, but it has some problems. The author evaluating the evidence may have a hard time keeping his or her own personal values, biases, and beliefs out of the evaluation. Or he or she may accidentally or intentionally leave out some portions of evidence that he or she does not agree with or finds problematic. Although this is an ideal way to make a great deal of information available to many people, it is difficult for the author to report fairly and accurately all that he or she examined.

The most important thing to remember when examining and evaluating evidence is that it needs to show you—rather than tell you—that the author's hypothesis is valid. The evidence Steiger and Woodward use to support their hypotheses must clearly show why their claims are valid. An author's supporting evidence is designed to show you that his or her hypothesis is logical. An author should not simply state his or her opinion that werewolves exist, for example. An author's opinion is no better than anyone else's. What you are looking for is whether the author can prove, or show you, that his or her opinion is valid based on some research or evidence. This would then demonstrate to you that the hypothesis is possible and that you should consider it worthwhile.

Now that you are familiar with some of the different types of evidence authors use, we will examine the work of both Steiger and Woodward and the ways in which they use evidence to support their hypotheses about the existence of werewolves.

Examining the Evidence Offered by Steiger

Steiger's hypothesis: The close relationship between humans and wolves has existed since the dawn of time; as such, it is not difficult to see the ways in which the primal nature of the modern-day serial killer resembles that of the traditional werewolf. In order to support his hypothesis, Steiger uses some evidence based on his own personal experience as a researcher and a writer on subjects dealing with the unexplained and the paranormal. Since we have already examined his credentials, we know that he brings a wealth of experience to the topic of werewolves. Thus, when he speaks about things he has learned through his own personal experiences, this is evidence worth considering valid.

In addition, Steiger refers to the research of experts in the fields of biology, psychology, demonic possession, and his own research into the field of werewolves. The references Steiger makes to the work of other professionals is accurately documented as published reports either within his text through appropriate citations or at the end of his encyclopedic entries in the form of bibliographical notes. These correct documentation methods demonstrate that Steiger is serious about the research he has conducted on his topic and is careful to include appropriate citations for his readers to check those sources themselves in case they either want to learn more about the topic or want to double-check his work.

Perhaps one element that may be lacking in Steiger's work is that he does not clearly show the relationship of his evidence to his main hypothesis. This can be problematic when you are evaluating arguments for your own research. The author bears the responsibility for proving his argument that werewolves exist. Although Steiger does present qualified examples to support his hypothesis, he fails to take the next step to illustrate *how* the examples prove his point. Thus, this leaves you with the job of drawing the connections and conclusions between elements of Steiger's argument.

Lacking an explicit explanation showing how the evidence illustrates the point of the hypothesis can be problematic in examining some forms of evidence, but it may not be entirely so in Steiger's case. The piece you are examining is from Steiger's *The Werewolf Book*, which is an encyclopedic collection of all that is known about werewolves. As a resource for potential evidence in developing an argument on a topic, an encyclopedia is generally not expected to provide in-depth, detailed analyses of how the information presented fits together. Thus, you may look at Steiger's work for the information it does provide without expecting too much from it. Is it a less valuable resource since it fails to include a more in-depth analysis of the evidence presented? Not necessarily. It depends on what you are looking for and how you will eventually use this piece of evidence to support your own argument about the existence of werewolves. Perhaps you might have certain ideas that werewolves can in fact be tied to serial killers and only need some specific examples to prove your own argument. In this case, Steiger's piece would be most helpful. But if you are still trying to work out the ways in which it is possible to think of serial killers as contemporary werewolves, then the lack of detailed analyses in

Steiger's piece may be more problematic for you. In this case, you might need to locate additional evidence that explains this connection in more detail. Interestingly, the references that Steiger supplies as bibliographical information might help you locate other sources of evidence that can explain these connections. Overall, though, the evidence Steiger presents does indeed support his hypothesis arguing for the existence of werewolves.

Examining the Evidence Offered by Woodward

Woodward's hypothesis: Eyewitness accounts of werewolves can be explained using scientific research that argues that those who were suspected of being werewolves really suffered from an acute case of rabies. In contrast to Steiger, Woodward uses more academic and scientific evidence to support his hypothesis that werewolves do not exist. Among these are eyewitness accounts, etymological analyses of word meanings, historical accounts, published reports (which, like Steiger, he carefully documents within the text), and expert opinion.

Woodward asserts that findings in biological and anthropological science can provide rational explanations, namely, recurring epidemics of human rabies, for the werewolves people claimed to have seen in eyewitness accounts. As evidence, Woodward refers to several accounts, describing in some detail the claims of eyewitnesses. He then goes on to provide a scientific explanation for each trait or symptom commonly assigned to werewolves and demonstrates their strong similarity to the symptoms and behaviors associated with individuals suffering from rabies. He also spends some time focusing on a detailed explanation of the ways in which rabies can be transmitted to humans, pointing out how these correlate with the ways in which humans were suspected of becoming werewolves. Using quotes from various fields of research, Woodward continues to demystify the werewolf. By analyzing historical documents (though he never says what these documents are), he demonstrates that epidemics of human rabies follow cyclical patterns that tend to coincide with the massive werewolf sightings that have been documented, particularly in eastern European history.

Overall, Woodward provides a great deal of evidence in very little space to support his hypothesis. Even though his professional credentials are sketchy, the intelligent and articulate way in which he handles the information may give you little doubt as to the accuracy and truth behind his research. However, thinking critically about the evidence Woodward provides yields some questions. For instance, how accurate is Woodward's interpretation of the research he presents? Since he relies heavily on a synthesis of a great deal of research into the subject of human rabies, you are forced to rely on his interpretation of the research for your information. Since he does not provide source information, except for several works from which he quotes directly, you have no way of checking the accuracy of his evaluations. This could be a problem if Woodward misrepresented his findings in the research or if he left out key points in the argument. Woodward might have strengthened his credibility if he had provided some additional references to allow you to do your own additional research on the topic or simply to check his.

In addition, since we lack solid information as to his professional credentials, we are not entirely certain that Woodward is himself an expert on the subject of werewolves. He occasionally gives his own opinion to prove his hypothesis that werewolves do not exist. As previously discussed, experts can be incorrect. The way Woodward has constructed his essay forces the reader to rely heavily on his methods of research and his own presumably expert opinion. Questioning Woodward on any of his points would force you to go out and do much of your own research on the topic to either prove Woodward wrong or to ensure the reliability of his research.

But does Woodward support his hypothesis? Absolutely! Ultimately, Woodward has given you a point-by-point explanation, supported by scientific, biological, and anthropological research, proving that eyewitness accounts of werewolves can be explained by natural or biological causes; thus, werewolves, as the eyewitnesses saw them, do not exist. Although you might have questions about how the evidence is handled, or whether Woodward's handling of it is thoroughly reliable, his piece is a successful example of how the evidence used needs to clearly support the hypothesis.

Step 4: Problems in Thinking About and Handling the Evidence

We have already discussed some of the difficulties that both Steiger and Woodward encounter in handling the evidence in support of their hypotheses. Before you practice evaluating one of the selections in this book on your own, you should be aware that authors encounter several specific problems when handling evidence that affect the strength of their argument and the final reliability of their work. It is the responsibility of the author, and the reader as well, to be highly aware of these difficulties. Awareness of the particular challenges faced by both the reader and the author allows both individuals a greater chance of arriving at a more certain conclusion to their original question—in our case, whether werewolves exist. We will look briefly at the types of problems involved with handling evidence.

Assumptions. Assumptions are statements accepted as true without proof. This problem is dangerous because the chances of being incorrect are high. Regarding whether werewolves exist, a writer might assume that werewolves are fiction and work only off of that assumption as opposed to conducting solid research that proves they are not real. Assumptions lack evidence to prove their accuracy.

Either/or perspective. This type of thinking argues that something is either black or white. This perspective does not allow for shades of gray or compromise or ambiguity. It is an extreme perspective with an all-or-nothing agenda that leaves no room for maybe, sometimes, or occasionally.

Absolutism. Absolutists have trouble seeing that there might be more than one way to look at the truth, that there are levels of complexity on certain issues that cannot be answered with a single *yes* or *no*. For example, an absolutist perspective on werewolves might be that werewolves absolutely do not exist in any way, shape, or form. This perspective would prevent the individual from seeing the alternative possibility that werewolves could exist in different forms and to varying degrees.

Biased viewpoints. To be biased is to be prejudiced toward a particular viewpoint. All people carry biases, some they are aware of and some they are not. In trying to develop a critical perspective, it is important to try to become aware of what your biases are. Also, you must ask questions about what the biases of the authors whose work you are evaluating might be. Bias affects the way you process and perceive information and events. It often prevents you from seeing what is reasonable or truthful in evidence simply because you are biased against it. On the other hand, bias can prompt you to see truth in something that is incorrect or inaccurate simply because it agrees with your views. In addition, bias prevents an author from fully considering other viewpoints since he or she might feel that his or her view is the only correct one.

Judgments based on double standards. Sometimes people use one set of rules or criteria to judge something they agree with and a completely different set of rules to judge something they disagree with. This is called holding a double standard. If an author believes that werewolves exist, he or she might hold evidence that argues for their existence to a different standard from evidence that proves that they do not exist. Fairness and objectivity demand that both sides of the argument be given equal treatment and analysis. Holding double standards prevents this from happening.

Jumping to conclusions. Sometimes readers and authors make a conclusion or judgment on a topic without enough information or evidence to ensure that the conclusion is correct. Reading only one article that argues for the existence of werewolves cannot provide enough evidence to conclude for certain that werewolves exist. There are other perspectives, other evidence, and other ideas that should be evaluated before making up your mind about something.

Overgeneralizing. Sometimes people draw broad conclusions or make wide judgments with only a small amount of evidence. For example, you may have read in one essay that werewolves can only transform at night when the moon is full. From this, you conclude that this must be true of all werewolves, but it may not be. You cannot be certain of this because you have not done the research to determine whether this is true of all werewolves. Overgeneralizing limits the ability of the reader or author to see the entire picture presented by the evidence, thus making an accurate conclusion impossible.

Stereotyping. A stereotype is really a type of overgeneralization that is fixed in the mind of the person who holds it and is resistant to change. It presents some of the same types of problems as overgeneralizations, but to a greater degree.

All of the challenges mentioned above prohibit clear and

critical thinking on a topic. They also prevent authors from thinking clearly about evidence and handling it appropriately in their writing. It is important to be aware that all people experience these barriers to critical thinking at various times, particularly when they hold strong feelings about a topic. Overcoming these barriers will enable you to more clearly see all of the possible perspectives related to an issue and to handle the evidence you gather more objectively as you search for answers. As you evaluate the evidence presented by the authors in this book, pay attention to these challenges. Do you see any biased perspectives? Are authors considering possibilities or viewpoints other than their own? Are they basing their arguments on stereotypes or overgeneralizations? Have they jumped to any conclusions that are not supported by appropriate evidence? Also pay attention to these questions in relation to your own evaluation of what the writers are presenting to you. Are you drawing conclusions based on clear and objective evaluations of the evidence, or are you allowing yourself to fall victim to the problems described above?

Step 5: Forming a Conclusion About the Author's Hypothesis

We have examined the hypotheses of Steiger and Woodward, evaluated the evidence presented by them in support of their hypotheses, and looked at some of the problems the authors encounter in thinking and writing critically about whether werewolves exist. It is time to form some conclusions about their hypotheses. Do they make sense? What do you think about the arguments presented by Steiger and Woodward? Who has a stronger case? What evidence have they presented that might help you to make up your mind about the existence of werewolves? Is their evidence alone enough for you to make a decision? Or do you need additional information before coming to a conclusion? Are your conclusions free of biases and stereotypes that might prevent you from clearly evaluating their evidence and making a solid judgment, even if that judgment opposes what you have always believed about werewolves?

Practice What You Have Learned

Select one or more of the remaining ten pieces from the book to evaluate on your own using the information in the steps outlined above. Since you are trying to answer whether werewolves exist, you might consider selecting one piece from each side of the argument and evaluating them next to each other. You can follow the format suggested below or make up one of your own. Just be sure to include all of the steps learned above.

Name of article_____ Author_____

1. Examine the author's background and experience. What credentials does the author hold that indicate whether she or he has some expertise in the field of werewolf or lycanthropy studies? How might the author's experiences or expertise present problems in how he or she perceives or handles evidence?

2. In one or two complete sentences, state the author's hypothesis in your own words. Be as specific as possible.

3a. In complete sentences, list the key points of evidence the author provides to support his or her hypothesis. You may want to create a numbered list as this will be easier to work with in the next step.

3b. Examine the evidence the author provides. For each key point of evidence you listed above, determine the type of evidence it is and evaluate whether it appears to be reliable and why. In general, do you believe the evidence provided by the author supports his or her hypothesis? Why or why not?

4. Consider the challenges the author may be dealing with in handling and presenting the evidence. Does there appear to be any hasty conclusions, stereotypes, or overgeneralizations? How might the author be overly biased toward his or her perspective? Also, consider whether you are experiencing any of these challenges yourself in examining the author's work. What biases do you hold toward the author's perspective? Are you evaluating each side of the argument equally, or are you evaluating the side that you agree with differently from the opposing side? Examine and discuss the problems these challenges present to both the author's ability to convince you of his hypothesis and your ability to think critically about the issue.

5. Form a conclusion about the writer's hypothesis. How has the writer used evidence to adequately support his or her claim? How does the author's argument assist you in determining the truth about werewolves? What conclusions can you reach about this mystery based on the author's hypothesis and evidence? Do you feel your question can be fully answered based on your evaluation, or do you need to do more research? Explain.

Note

1. For a more detailed discussion of the key terms and concepts related to the types and handling of evidence, as well as additional strategies for developing critical-thinking skills, please see Vincent Ryan Ruggiero, *Beyond Feelings: A Guide to Critical Thinking*, 6th ed. Columbus, OH: Mayfield, 2001.

Glossary

berserk: A Viking warrior who attacked with a crazed fury.

incubus: An evil spirit that lies atop persons in their sleep, especially a spirit that is believed to have sexual intercourse with women while they are sleeping.

loup-garou: A French term meaning "werewolf."

lycanthropist: One who suffers from the disease of lycanthropy.

lycanthropy: A delusion that one has become a wolf; taking on the form and characteristics of a wolf by witchcraft or magic.

porphyria: A metabolic blood disorder, usually hereditary, that may cause sensitivity to light, abdominal cramping, and the appearance of particular chemicals, called porphyrins, in the blood and urine, which cause the urine to turn purple.

transmogrify: To change or alter greatly and often with grotesque or humorous effect.

warlock: A man who practices the black arts of magic; a male witch.

werewolf disease: Refers to the mental condition of lycanthropy, in which a patient experiences the delusion that he or she is a werewolf.

For Further Research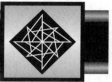

Books

Leonard R.N. Ashley, *The Complete Book of Werewolves*. Fort Lee, NJ: Barricade Books, 2001.

Thomas G. Aylesworth, *Werewolves and Other Monsters*. Reading, MA: Addison-Wesley, 1971.

Daniel Cohen, *Werewolves*. New York: Cobblehill, 1996.

Douglas Drake, *Horror!* New York: Collier Books, 1966.

Katherine Edwards, ed., *Werewolves, Witches, and Wandering Spirits: Traditional Belief and Folklore in Early Modern Europe*. Kirksville, MT: Truman State University Press, 2002.

Robert Eisler, *Man into Wolf*. Santa Barbara, CA: Ross-Erikson, 1978.

Nancy Garden, *Werewolves*. Philadelphia: J.B. Lippincott, 1973.

Clemence Houseman, *The Were-wolf*. New York: Arno, 1976.

Bernhardt J. Hurwood, *Vampires, Werewolves, and Ghouls*. New York: Ace Books, 1968.

Richard Noll, *Bizarre Diseases of the Mind*. New York: Berkley Books, 1990.

Elliott O'Donnell, *Werewolves*. London: Methuen, 1912.

Brad Steiger, *Demon Lovers: Cases of Possession, Vampires, and Werewolves*. New Brunswick, NJ: Inner Light, 1987.

Periodicals

Thomas Fahy et al., "Werewolves, Vampires, and Cannibals," *Medicine, Science, and the Law*, April 1988.

Lee Illis, "On Porphyria and the Aetiology of Werewolves," *Proceedings of the Royal Society of Medicine*, 1964.

H.A. Rosenstock and K.R. Vincent, "A Case of Lycanthropy," *American Journal of Psychiatry*, 1977.

Harry Senn, "Romanian Werewolves: Seasons, Rituals, Cycles," *Folklore*, 1982.

Internet Source

Paula Gunn, "The Werewolf: A Monster for a New Millennium." www.darkecho.com. This essay, written by a respected Native American author, analyzes the evolution of the werewolf and its increasing popularity.

Websites

Legend of the Werewolf: Fact or Fiction?, www.angelfire.com/ny/brandybean/index3.html. This site briefly addresses the key elements of the mythology surrounding the werewolf.

Occultopedia, www.occultopedia.com. An encyclopedia of the unexplained, the occult, mythology, and other mysteries of the paranormal.

The Shapeshifter and Werewolf Handbook, www.lycanthrope.org. This site presents a large database of questions, answers, and facts pertaining to werewolves.

Werewolfpage.com, www.werewolfpage.com. A collection of resources and links about the legend of the werewolf.

Werewolves-Lycanthropy, www.crystalinks.com/werewolves.html. This site provides an extensive glossary of terms and definitions as well as a complete historical chronology of the werewolf.

Index

Roulet, Jacques, 83–84
Russia, 96

sadism, 110–11, 140
Sailors' Union of the Pacific, 63
Satan, 54, 80
  influence over werewolves, 20,
    42–43, 45, 108
  through application of
    salves, 21, 25–26, 46, 139
  witches and, 44, 48–49
Scarver, Christopher, 61
schizophrenia. *See* mental illness
Scotland, 33–35
Scott, Sir Walter, 98, 99
sensitivity, to light, 102, 103
serial killers, 14, 15, 55
  characteristics of lycanthropy
    common among, 11–12
  see also Dahmer, Jeffrey;
    Gordon, Harry
sex criminals, 57–58, 60, 62–65
sexuality, 117, 124, 130, 134–35,
  143
Shipley Hartford tests, 145–46
Sidetes, Marcellus, 112
skin disorders, 103
Spina, Fra Bartolomeo, 47–48
Sponde, Jean de, 45–46, 139–40
Steiger, Brad, 11, 55
Stoker, Bram, 82
strychnine, 146
suicide, 39
Summers, Montague, 42, 139
supernatural, the, 7, 50, 58, 93
  see also possession, demonic;
    Satan
*Supernatural: Vampires, Zombies
  and Monster Men, The* (Farson),
  82
Surawicz, Frida G., 122, 123,
  127, 137
swan-maidens, 108
Switzerland, 95

Texas, 65
Thomas, Saint, 48

Thyraeus, Peter, 139
Toole, Otis Elwood, 65
transformation, 9–12, 14, 42–46,
  52–54, 86–87
  black magic and, 51, 98
  controversy regarding, 8, 108
  delusions of, 13, 99, 124, 127
    triggered by dreams, 109–10
    triggered by drugs, 141
  demonic possession and, 47
  dreams of, 89
  of gods and heroes in
    mythology, 87
  during hours of darkness, 85
    sensitivity to light and, 103
  involuntary, 66, 72–73,
    116–17
  during childhood, 67–70
  fear and, 71, 75
  feelings of rage and, 69, 74
  involvement of devil in, 51–54
    through application of salve,
      21, 25–26, 46, 139
  key element of werewolf
    phenomenon, 15
  lycanthropy sufferer's belief in,
    24
  nakedness and, 22
  physical nature of, 43
  supernatural nature of, 50
  variety of beliefs concerning
    causes of, 7
  voluntary, 58
  of women, 100, 108
  into cats, 44, 48–49
treatment, for lycanthropy,
  38–40, 140
trials, 23–24, 44, 52, 83–84, 103
  serial killer's courtroom
    statement and, 61
Turkey, 96

University of Kentucky Medical
  College, 137

Vampire in Legend, Fact, and Art
  (Copper), 97